CREATIVE PARENTING
Made Easier: From Infant to Teenager to Adulthood

Travis W. Royal

Publisher's Cataloging-in-Publication
(Provided by Quality Books, Inc.)

Creative Parenting made easier: from infant to teenager to adulthood/
    edited by Travis W. Royal -- 1st ed.
    P.cm.
    Includes bibligraphical references.
    LCCN: 97-94195
    ISBN: 0-9659730-0-X

    1. Child rearing. 2. Parenting. 3. Education
    -- Parent participation. I. Royal, Travis W.
HQ769.C74 2000   649.1
                            QB199-1317

Printed in the United States of America

**ATTENTION COLLEGES AND UNIVERSITIES, COPORATIONS,
AND PROFESSIONAL ORGANIZATIONS:** Quality discounts are
available on bulk purchases of this book for educational training purposes,
gift giving or fund raising. Special books, book excerpts or booklets can
also be created to fit your specific needs. For information, contact
Marketing Department, Missy Merchandise Publications, P.O. Box 13351,
Fort Wayne, Indiana 46856 or call (800) 973-7988 Fax: (219) 744-9721
Email: TROYAL 1001@AOL.COM

CONTENTS

Acknowledgments

This book would never have been possible without the skillful prose and hard work of the Food Safety and Inspection Service who asked food scientists to analyze consumer handling of food in the home using HACCP (Hazard Analysis and Critical Control Point) approach. This section, the result of that effort, guides you past those critical points in everyday food handling where experts say making the "wrong" move could lead to foodborne illness.

Thanks go out to the Department of Health and Human Services who provided critical information on Preventing Childhood Poisonings.

Thanks go out to the National Institute of Mental Health (NIMH), the Federal Agency that supports research nationwide on the brain, mental illnesses, and mental health.

Assistance was also provided by staff from the National Clearinghouse for Alcohol and Drug Information, the National Institute on Drug Abuse, and by consultants Elizabeth S. McConnell and Joel M. Moskowitz.

Other contributing organizations include: the American Federation of Teachers, the Far West Laboratory for Educational Research and Development, and the North Central Regional Educational Laboratory.

Particularly, I would like to acknowledge my parents, Betty L. Royal and William H. Royal and family for their wisdom, love, and support.

But above all I would like to thank GOD for granting me the serenity to accept the things I cannot change, the courage to change the things I can and the wisdom to know the difference.

- PRAYER OF SERENITY

Part 1
Baby Safety Checklist

In The Bedroom:

Put your baby to sleep on her back or side in a crib with a flat, firm mattress and no soft bedding underneath her. Follow this advice to reduce the risk of suffocation and Sudden Infant Death Syndrome (SIDS). To prevent suffocation, never put babies to sleep on adult beds. Make sure your baby's crib is sturdy and has no loose or missing hardware. This will prevent babies suffocating or strangling by becoming trapped between broken crib parts.

Never place your baby's crib or furniture near window blind or curtain cords. This will prevent babies from strangling on the loop of the cord. To prevent falls, keep children away from windows.

In The Bathroom:

Keep medicines and cleaning products in containers with safety caps and locked away from children. This will prevent children from being poisoned.

Always check bath water temperature with your wrist or elbow before putting your baby in to bathe. This will prevent burns to baby's delicate skin.

Never, ever, leave your child alone in the bathtub or near any water. This will prevent children from drowning. In addition, keep children away all standing water, including water in toilets, 5-gallon buckets, and pools.

In The Kitchen:

Don't leave your baby alone in a highchair; always use all safety straps. This will prevent injuries and deaths from the baby climbing out, falling, or sliding under the tray. Be sure to use safety straps in strollers and baby swings.

Use, your stove's back burners and keep pot handles turned to the back of the stove, This will prevent deaths and injuries from burns. In addition, keep children away from tablecloths, so they can't pull down hot foods or liquids on themselves.

Lock household cleaning products, knives, matches, and plastic bags away from children. This will prevent poisoning, bleeding injuries, burns, and suffocation.

In other living areas:

Install smoke detectors on each floor of your home, especially near sleeping areas; change the batteries yearly. This will prevent deaths and injuries from falls and electric shocks.

Use safety gates to block stairways and safety plugs to cover electrical outlets. This will prevent injuries from falls and electric shocks.

Keep all small objects, including tiny toys and balloons, away from young children. This will prevent choking and possible death.

Part 2
Consumer Guide To Safe Food Handling

This section tells you what to do at each step in food handling — from shopping through storing leftovers — to avoid food poisoning.

Never had food poisoning? Actually, it's called foodborne illness. Perhaps you have, but thought you were sick with the flu. Some 33 million Americans could suffer from foodborne illness this year.

Why? Because under the right conditions, bacteria you can't see, smell or taste can make you sick.

It doesn't have to happen, through. Many such cases could be avoided if people just handled food properly. So here's what to do...

When You Shop:

1. Buy cold food last, get it home fast.
2. When you're out, grocery shop last. Take food straight home to the refrigerator. Never leave food in a hot car!
3. Don't buy anything you won't use before the use-by date.
4. Don't buy food in poor condition. Make sure refrigerated food is cold to the touch. Frozen food should be rock-solid. Canned goods should be free of dents, cracks or bulging lids, which can indicate a serious food poisoning threat.

When You Store Food:

Check the temperature of your refrigerator with an appliance thermometer. To keep bacteria in check, the refrigerator should run at 40° F; the freezer unit at 0° F. Keep your refrigerator as cold as possible without freezing milk or lettuce.

1. Freeze fresh meat, poultry or fish immediately if you can't use it within a few days.
2. Put packages of raw meat, poultry or fish on a plate before refrigerating so their juices won't drip on other food. Raw juices often contain bacteria.

When You Prepare Food:

1. Keep everything clean. Thaw in refrigerator.
2. Wash hands in hot soapy water before preparing food and after using the bathroom,

changing diapers and handling pets.

3. Harmful bacteria multiply quickly in kitchen towels, sponges and cloths. Wash cloth items often in hot-cycle in your machine. Consider using paper towels to clean up meat and poultry juices. Avoid sponges or place them in the dishwasher daily to kill bacteria.

4. Keep raw meat, poultry and fish and their juices away from other food. For instance, wash your hands, cutting board, knife and countertops in hot soapy water after cutting up the chicken and before slicing salad ingredients. Also use hot soapy water to wash sink and kitchen faucet handles the raw meat or your "meat-covered" hands have touched.

5. Use plastic or other non-porous cutting boards rather than wooden ones. These boards should be run through the dishwasher after use.

6. What about antibacterial sanitizers in the kitchen? Food handling experts feel hot soapy water used properly should protect you adequately against foodborne bacteria. However, kitchen sanitizers (including a mixture of bleach and water) can provide some added protection. NOTE: Sanitizer product directions must be followed carefully as products differ greatly.

7. Thaw frozen food in the refrigerator or in the microwave, NOT on the kitchen counter. Marinate in the refrigerator too.

When You're Cooking:

It takes thorough cooking to kill harmful bacteria, so you're taking chances when you eat meat, poultry, fish or eggs that are raw or only partly cooked. Plus, hamburger that is red in the middle and rare steak and roast beef are also undercooked from the safety standpoint.

1. Generally cook red meat to 160° F. Cook poultry to 180° F. Use a meat thermometer to check that it's cooked all the way through.

2. To check visually, red meat is done when it's brown or grey inside. Poultry juices run clear. Fish flakes with a fork.

3. Ground meat, where bacteria can spread throughout the meat during processing,

should be cooked to at least 160° F. This means there is no pink left in the middle or in juices. You can allow large cuts like roasts to stay slightly pink in the center as long as they've reached at least 145° F (medium-rare). Do not serve any cut at this low temperature if you have scored (cut or poked with a fork) or tenderized it before cooking, thus forcing surface bacteria into the center.

4. Salmonella, a bacteria that a causes food poisoning, can grow inside fresh, unbroken eggs. So cook eggs until the yolk and white are firm, not runny. Scramble eggs to a firm texture. Don't use recipes in which eggs remain raw or only partially cooked.

Safe Microwaving:

A great timesaver, the microwave has one food safety disadvantage. It sometimes leaves cold spots in food. Bacteria can survive in these spots. So...

1. Cover food with a lid or plastic wrap so steam can aid thorough cooking Vent wrap to make sure it doesn't touch the food.

2. Stir and rotate your food for even cooking. No turntable? Rotate the dish by hand once or twice during cooking.

3. Observe the standing time called for in recipe or package directions. During the standing time, food finishes cooking.

4. Use the oven temperature probe or a meat thermometer to check that food is done. Insert it at several spots.

When You Serve Food:

1. Use clean dishes and utensils to serve food, not those used in preparation. Serve grilled food on a clean plate too, not one that held raw meat, poultry or fish.

2. Never leave perishable food out of the refrigerator over 2 hours! Bacteria that can cause food poisoning grow quickly at warm temperatures.

3. Pack lunches in insulated carriers with a cold pack. Caution children never to leave lunches in direct sun or on a warm radiator.

4. Carry picnic food in a cooler with a cold pack. When possible, put the cooler in the shade. Keep the lid on as much as you can.

5. Party time? Keep cold party food on ice or serve it throughout the gathering from platters from the refrigerator.

    Likewise, divide hot party food into smaller serving platters. Keep platters refrigerated until time to warm them up for serving.

When You Handle Leftovers:

1. Divide large amounts of leftovers into small, shallow containers for quick cooling in the refrigerator. Don't pack the refrigerator — cool air must circulate to keep food safe.

2. With poultry or other stuffed meats, remove stuffing and refrigerate it in separate containers.

Reheating:

1. Bring sauces, soups and gravy to a boil. Heat other leftovers thoroughly to 165° F.

2. Microwave leftovers using a lid or vented plastic wrap for thorough heating.

Kept It Too Long?

Safe refrigerator and freezer storage time-limits are given for many common foods in the "Cold Storage" table in the following section. But what about something you totally forgot about and may have kept too long?

1. When in doubt, throw it out.

2. Danger — never taste food that looks or smells strange to see if you can still use it. Just discard it.

3. Is it moldy? The mold you see is only the tip of the iceberg. The poisons molds can form are found under the surface of the food. So, While you can sometimes save hard cheese and salamis and firm fruits and vegetables by cutting the mold out — remove a large area around it, most moldy food should be discarded.

Cold Storage:

Product	Refrigerator (40° F)	Freezer (0° F)
Eggs		
Fresh, in shell	3 weeks	Don't freeze
Raw yolks, whites	2-4 days	1 year
Hardcooked	1 week	Don't freeze well
Liquid pasteurized or		
egg substitutes, opened	3 days	Don't freeze
unopened	10 days	1 year

Product	Refrigerator (40° F)	Freezer (0° F)
Mayonnaise, commercial		
Refrigerate after opening	2 months	Don't freeze
TV Dinners, Frozen Casseroles		
Keep frozen until ready to serve		3-4 months
Deli & Vacuum-Packed Products		
Store-prepared (or homemade) egg, chicken, tuna, ham, macaroni salads	3-5 days	
Pre-stuffed pork & lamb chops,		
Chicken breast stuffed with dressing	1 day	These products don't freeze well
Store-cooked convenience meals	1-2 days	
Commercial brand vacuum-packed	2 weeks	
Dinners with USDA seal	unopened	
Soups & Stews		
Vegetable or meat-added	3-4 days	2-3 months
Hamburger, Ground & Stew Meals		
Hamburger & stew meats	1-2 days	3-4 months
Ground turkey, veal, pork, lamb & mixtures of them	1-2 days	3-4 months
Hotdogs & Lunch Meats		
Hotdogs, opened package	1 week	
unopened package	2 weeks	In freezer wrap
Lunch meats, opened	3-5 days	1-2 months
unopened	2 weeks	

Note: These SHORT but safe time limits will help keep refrigerated food from spoiling or becoming dangerous to eat. These time limits will keep frozen food at top quality.

Product	Refrigerator (40° F)	Freezer (0° F)
Bacon & Sausage		
Bacon 7 days	1 month	
Sausage, raw from pork, beef, turkey	1-2 days	1-2 months
Smoked breakfast links, patties	7 days	1-2 months
Hard sausage -- pepperoni, jerky sticks	2-3 weeks	1-2 months
Ham, Corn Beef		
Corn beef drained or wrapped in pouch with pickling juices	5-7 days	1 month
Ham, canned		
Label says keep refrigerated	6-9 months	Don't freeze
Ham, fully cooked – whole	7 days	1-2 months
Ham, fully cooked – half	3-5 days	1-2 months
Ham, fully cooked – slices	3-4 days	1-2 months
Fresh Meat		
Steaks, beef	3-5 days	6-12 months
Chop, pork	3-5 days	4-6 months
Chop, lamb	3-5 days	6-9 months
Roast, beef	3-5 days	6-12 months
Roast, lamb	3-5 days	6-9 months

Roast, pork & veal	3-5 days	4-6 months
Variety meats - Tongue, brain, kidneys, liver, heart, chitterlings	1-2 days	3-4 months
Meat Leftovers		
Cooked meat and meat dishes	3-4 days	2-3 months
Gravy and meat broth	1-2 days	2-3 months
Fresh Poultry		
Chicken or turkey, whole	1-2 days	1 year
Chicken or turkey pieces	1-2 days	9 months
Giblets	1-2 days	3-4 months
Cooked Poultry, Leftover		
Fried chicken	3-4 days	4 months
Cooked poultry dishes	3-4 days	4-6 months
Pieces, plain	3-4 days	4 months
Pieces covered with broth, gravy	1-2 days	6 months
Chicken nuggets, patties	1-2 days	1-3 months

Cooking Temperatures

Product	Fahrenheit
Eggs & Egg Dishes	
Egg	Cook until yolk & white are firm
Egg dishes	160°
Ground Meat & Meat Mixture	
Turkey, chicken	165°
Veal, beef, lamb, pork	160°
Fresh beef	
Medium Rare	145°
Medium	160°
Well Done	170°
Fresh Veal	
Medium Rare	145°
Medium	160°
Well Done	170°
Fresh Lamb	
Medium Rare	145°
Medium	160°
Well Done	170°
Fresh Pork	
Medium	160°
Well Done	170°

Power's Out
Your Freezer:

With power, a full upright or chest freezer will keep everything frozen for about 2 days. A half-full freezer will keep food frozen 1 day.

If power will be coming back on fairly soon, you can make the food last longer by keeping the door shut as much as possible.

If power will be off for an extended period, take food to friend freezers, locate a commercial freezer or use dry ice.

Your Refrigerator-Freezer Combination:

Without power, the refrigerator section will keep food cool 4-6 hours depending on the kitchen temperature.

A full, well-functioning freezer unit should keep food frozen for 2 days. A half-full freeze unit should keep things frozen about 1 day.

Block ice can keep food on the refrigerator shelves cooler. Dry ice

Poultry

Chicken, whole	180°
Turkey, whole	180°
Poultry breasts, roasts	170°
Poultry thighs, wings	Cook until juices run clear
Stuffing (cooked alone or in bird)	165°
Duck & Goose	180°

Ham

Fresh (raw)	160°
Pre-cooked (to reheat)	140°

can be added to the freezer unit. You can't touch dry ice and you shouldn't breathe the fumes, so follow handling instructions carefully.

Thawed Food?

Food still containing ice crystals or that feels refrigerator-cold can be frozen.

Discard any thawed food that has risen to room temperature and remained there 2 hours or more. Immediately discard anything with a strange color or odor.

Is It Food Poisoning?

If you or your family member develop nausea, vomiting, diarrhea, fever or cramps, you could have food poisoning. Unfortunately, it's not always easy to tell since, depending on the illness, symptoms can appear anywhere from 30 minutes to 2 weeks after eating bad food. Most often, though, people get sick within 4 to 48 hours after eating.

In more serious cases, food poisoning victims may have nervous system problems like paralysis, double vision or trouble swallowing or breathing. If symptoms are severe or the victim is very young, old, pregnant, or already ill, call a doctor or go to the doctor right away.

When To Report Foodborne Illness:

You or your physician should report serious cases of food borne illness to the local health department. Report any food poisoning incidents if the food involved came from a restaurant or commercial outlet.

Give a detailed, but short account of the incident. If the food is a commercial product, have it in hand so you can describe it over the phone.

If you're asked to keep the food refrigerated so officials can examine it later, follow directions carefully.

For more information on food handling, call USDA's Meat and Poultry Hotline **(800-535-4555)** 10-4 weekdays Eastern Time.

Part 3
Learn How To Protect Your Child
Against Other Types Of Poisons

Poison-Proofing Your Home:

Poison-proofing your home is the key to preventing childhood poisoning. Always close the container as soon as you've finished using it. Properly secure the child-resistant packaging, and put it away immediately in a place where children can't reach it.

Lead Poisoning:

Although lead levels in food and drink are the lowest in history, concern remains about lead leaching into food from ceramic ware. Improperly fired or formulated glazes on ceramic ware can allow lead to leach into food or drink.

Long recognized as a toxic substance, adverse health effects can result from exposure to lead over months or years.

After a California family suffered acute lead poisoning in 1969 from drinking orange juice stored in a pitcher bought in Mexico, FDA established "action levels" for lead in ceramic ware used to serve food. Over the years, these original action levels have been revised as research has shown that exposure to even small amounts of lead can be hazardous. The last revision for ceramic foodware was in 1991. On Jan.12, 1994, FDA published a regulation for decorative ceramic ware not intended for food use, requiring a permanently affixed label on high-lead leaching products.

"Most lead toxicity comes from multiple exposure and is a slow accumulation over time," says Robert Mueller, nurse and poison information specialist at the Virginia Poison Center, headquartered at the Medical College of Virginia Hospitals in Richmond. "Refusing to eat, vomiting, convulsions, and malaise can all be symptoms of lead poisoning." Because lead poisoning occurs over time, such symptoms may not show up right away. A blood test is the surest way to determine that your child has not been exposed to significant amounts of lead.

"In general, if a consumer purchases ceramic ware in the U.S. marketplace today, it meets the new action levels," says Julia Hewgley, public affairs specialist with FDA's

Center for Food Safety and Applied Nutrition. "But if you travel abroad and buy ceramic ware, be aware that each country has its own safety regulations. Safety can be terribly variable depending on the type of quality control and whether the piece is made by a hobbyist." To guard against poisonings, Hewgley advises that ceramic ware not be used to store foods. Acidic foods — such as orange, tomato and other fruits, tomato sauces, vinegar, and wine — stored in improperly glazed containers are potentially the most dangerous. Frequently used products, like cups or pitchers, are also potentially danger-ous, especially when used to hold hot, acidic foods.

"Stop using any item if the glaze shows a dusty or chalky gray residue after washing. Limit-your use of antique or collectable housewares for food and beverages," she says.

"Buy one of the quick tests available at hardware stores and do a screening on inher-ited pieces."

Iron Poisoning:

Iron-containing products remain the biggest problem by far when it comes to child-hood poisoning. In October 1994, FDA proposed regulations for unit-dose packaging requirements for iron containing products with 30 milligrams or more of iron per dosage unit. The agency also proposed requiring warning labels about the adverse effects of high dose iron ingestion by children for all iron-containing products taken in solid oral dosage forms. Because of the time and effort needed to open unit-dose products, FDA believes unit-dose packaging will discourage a youngster, or at least limit the number of tablets a child would swallow, reducing the potential for serious illness or death.

FDA's proposed requirements would be in addition to existing U.S. Consumer Prod-uct Safety Commission regulations, which require child-resistant packaging for most iron- containing products was expected soon.

Iron is an essential nutrient sometimes lacking in people's diets which is why iron is often recommended for people with conditions such as iron-deficiency anemia. Taken as indicated, iron is safe. But when tablets are taken beyond the proper dose in a short period, especially by toddlers or infants, serious injury or death may result.

Children poisoned with iron face immediate and long-term problems. Within minutes or hours of swallowing iron tablets, nausea, vomiting, diarrhea, and gastrointestinal bleeding can occur. These problems can progress to shock, coma, seizures, and death. Even if a child appears to have no symptoms after accidentally swallowing irons or appears to be recovering, medical evaluation should still be sought since successful treatment is difficult once iron is absorbed from the small intestine into the bloodstream. And children who survive iron poisoning can experience other problems, such as gastrointestinal obstruction and liver damage, up to four after the ingested poisoning.

FDA regulates iron-containing products as either drugs or foods, depending on the product formulation and on intended use, as defined by labeling and other information sources. Iron products are regulated as drugs if they are intended to affect the structure or function of the body, or are used in the diagnosis, cure, treatment, or prevention of disease and are listed in the U.S. Pharmacopeia. All other products are regulated as foods.

Some iron-containing products have been regulated as prescription drugs because they included pharmacologic doses of folic acid and usually were prescribed to meet high nutritional requirements during pregnancy,

Between June 1992 and January 1993, five toddlers died after eating iron supplement tablets, according to the National Centers for Disease Control and Prevention's Morbidity and Mortality Weekly Report of Feb. 19, 1993. All tablets involved in the reported deaths were prenatal iron supplements. The incidents, occurred in a variety of ways: Children ate tablets from uncapped or loosely capped bottles, swallowed tablets found spilled on the floor, and in one case, a 2-year-old fed an 11-month-old sibling tablets from a box found on the floor.

Iron is always included in prenatal vitamins prescribed for pregnant women, and is sometimes included in multivitamin formulas. Often available without prescription, iron supplements can be found in grocery stores, drugstores, and health food stores in a wide variety of potencies, ranging from 18 milligrams (mg) to 150 mg per pill. For a small child, as little as 600 mg of iron can be fatal.

Because iron supplements are typically brightly colored and may look like candy,

they are particularly attractive to children. In 1993, the Nonprescription Drug Manufacturers Association (NDMA), which manufactures about 95 percent of nonprescription
OTC medicines available to Americans today, adopted formulation provisions for iron
products containing 30 mg or more of elemental iron per solid dosage form. These provisions also stipulated that such products would not be made with coatings. That same
year, NDMA manufacturers also independently agreed to develop new voluntary warning labels far those products. The voluntary labels read: "Warning: Close tightly and
keep out of reach of children. Contains iron, which can be harmful or fatal to children in
large doses. In case of accidental overdose, seek professional assistance or contact a
poison control center immediately."

Signs of Poisoning:

How can you tell if your child has ingested something poisonous? "Most poisons,
with the exception of lead, work fairly quickly. A key is when the child was otherwise
well and in a space of hours develops unusual symptoms: They can't follow you with
their eyes, they're sleepy before it's their naptime, their eyes go around in circles. Any
unusual or new symptoms should make you think of poisoning as a possibility," Rodgers
advises. "Poisonings typically affect the stomach and central nervous system. If a child
suddenly throws up that can be more difficult to diagnose."

Other signs of poison ingestion can be burns around the lips or mouth, stains of the
substance around the child's mouth, or the smell of a child's breath. Suspect a possible
poisoning if you find an open or spilled bottle of pills.

If you suspect poisoning, remain calm. For medicines, call the nearest poison control center or your physician. For household chemical ingestion, follow first-aid instructions on the label, and. then call the poison center or your doctor. When you call, tell
them your child's age, height and weight, existing health conditions as much as you
know about the substance involved, the exposure route (swallow? inhaled? splashed in
the eyes?), and if your child has vomited. If you know what substance the child has
ingested, take the remaining solution or bottle with you to the phone when you call.
Follow the instructions of the poison control center precisely.

Progress Against Poisonings:

The nation's first poison control center opened in Chicago in 1953, after a study of accidental deaths in childhood reported a large number were due to poisoning. Since that time, a combination of public education, the use of child-resistant caps, help through poison control centers, and increased sophistication in medical care have lowered overall death rates.

Often, calling a poison center simply reassures parents that the product ingested is not poisonous. In other cases, following phone instructions prevents an emergency room trip.

Children are not the only victims of accidental poisonings: Older people in particular are at risk because they generally take more medicines, may have problems reading labels correctly, or may take a friend's or spouse's medicine.

In June 1995, the U.S. Consumer Product Safety Commission voted unanimously to require that child-resistant caps be made so adults - especially senior citizens - will have a less frustrating time getting them off. Because many adults who had trouble with child-resistant caps left them off, or transferred their contents to less secure packaging that endangers children, officials say the new caps will be safer for children.

"Childhood poisoning will always be a focus, because children are so vulnerable, especially children under age 5," says Ken Giles, public affairs spokesman for the Consumer Product Safety Commission. "The first two or three years of a child's life are the highest-risk time for all kinds of injuries, so there is a special need to educate new parents. It's essential we keep raising these safety messages that medicines and chemicals can be poisonous."

Antidotes:

If you suspect childhood poisoning, call the nearest poison control center or your physician first, and follow their instructions precisely.

To induce vomiting in case of accidental poisoning, experts recommend keeping on hand syrup of ipecac-safely stored away from children, of course! Syrup of ipecac induces vomiting, thus ridding the body of the swallowed poison. It usually works within a half-hour of ingestion.

Some medical experts also recommend that parents keep activated charcoal on hand as well: You may have to ask your druggist for it, because it may not be on store shelves. Although some poison control experts recommend having activated charcoal on hand, there is a difference of opinion on its use by consumers. The U.S. Consumer Product Safety Commission, for example, does not recommend that consumers use activated charcoal because it is less palatable to young children.

Activated charcoal (or charcoal treated with substances that increase its absorption abilities) absorbs poison, preventing it from spreading throughout the body. One advantage of activated charcoal is that it can be effective for a considerable time after the poison is swallowed. But activated charcoal should never be used at the same time you administer syrup of ipecac: The charcoal will absorb the ipecac.

For children ages 1 to 12, give one tablespoon of syrup of ipecac followed by one or two glasses of water. Children ages 12 and over should get two tablespoons, followed by one or two glasses of water.

Activated charcoal is usually found in drugstores in liquid form in 30-gram doses. For children under 5, give one gram per every two pounds of body weight. Older children and adults may require much higher doses.

Both antidotes should only be used on conscious poison victims; an unconscious victim should always be treated by professionals.

"Remember to call your local poison control center first before giving your child any at-home antidote," says-Robert Mueller, poison information, specialist at the Virginia Poison Center in Richmond, Va.

Protect Yourself Against Medicine Tampering:

With FDA's new proposed regulations regarding packaging of high-dose, iron-containing pills in mind, it's important to remember that no packaging or warnings can protect without your involvement. Nonprescription OTC drugs sold in the United States are among the most safely packaged consumer products in the world, but "child-resistant" and "tamperresistant" do not mean "childproof" and "tamperproof."

FDA adopted "tamper-resistant" packaging requirements after seven people in the Chicago area died from taking cyanide-laced Extra-Strength Tylenol capsules in 1982. Although the product met all FDA requirements at the time, it wasn't designed so tampering would leave visible evidence. FDA swiftly enacted new regulations requiring most OTC drug products to be packaged in "tamper-resistant" packaging, defined as "packaging having an indicator or barrier to entry that could reasonable be expected to provide visible evidence that tampering had occurred," and required OTC product labeling to alert consumers to tamper-resistant packaging. In 1989, FDA regulations were amended to require two-piece hard gelatin capsules to be packaged using at least two tamper-resistant features unless sealed with a tamper-resistant technology.

"Consumer vigilance is part of the equation," says Lana Ragazinsky, consumer safety officer with FDA's Center for Drug Evaluation and Research, Division of Drug Quality Evaluation, Office of Compliance. "The consumer is being led into a false sense of security because they see 'tamper-resistant'... 'Tamper evident' means you, the consumer, need to look for evidence of tampering."

FDA has proposed changing the term "tamper-resistant" to "tamper-evident" to underscore the fact that no package design is tamperproof. The most important tool to detect tampering is you! Here are a few tips to help protect against tampering:

1. Read the label. OTC medicines with tamper-evident packages tell you what seals and features to look for.

2. Inspect the outer packaging before you buy.

3. Inspect the medicine when you open the package, and look again before you take it. If it looks suspicious: be suspicious.

4. Look for capsules or tablets different in any way from others in the package.

5. Don't use any medicine from a package with cuts, tears, slices, or other imperfections.

6. Never take medicine in the dark. Read the label and look at the medicine every time you take a dose.

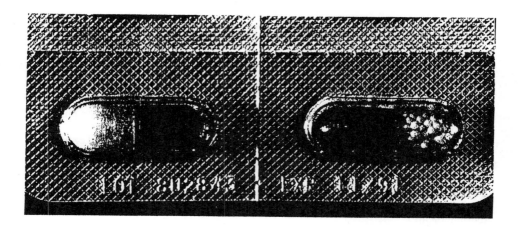

Close visual examination can often expose tampering. In this blisterpack, the capsule on the left contains cyanide, a yellowish powder that does not resemble the larger white, time release beads in the untouched Sudafed capsule on the right. These capsules are from the 1991 Sudafed tampering case in Washington state.

Part 4
Learning Disabilities

Imagine having important needs and ideas to communicate, but being unable to express them. Perhaps feeling bombarded by sights and sounds, unable to focus your attention. Or trying to read or add but not being able to make sense of the letters or numbers.

You may not need to imagine. You may be the parent or teacher of a child experiencing academic problems, or have someone in your family diagnosed as learning disabled. Or possibly as a child you were told you had a reading disorder called dyslexia or some other handicap.

Although different from person to person, these difficulties make up the common daily experiences of many learning disabled children, adolescents, and adults. A person with a learning disability may experience a cycle of academic failure and lowered self-esteem. Having these handicaps — or living with someone who has them — can bring overwhelming frustration.

But the prospects are hopeful. It is important to remember that a person with a learning disability can learn. The disability usually only affects certain limited areas of a child's development. In fact, rarely are learning disabilities severe enough to impair a person's potential to live a happy, normal life.

According to the National Institute of Mental Health (NIMH), the Federal agency that supports research nationwide on the brain, mental illnesses, and mental health, scientists supported by NIMH are dedicated to understanding the workings and interrelationships of the various regions of the brain, and to finding preventions and treatments to overcome brain dysfunctions that handicap people in school, work, and play.

This book also provides up-to date information on learning disabilities and the role of NIMH-sponsored research in discovering underlying causes and effective treatments. It describes treatment options, strategies for coping, and sources of information and support, Among these sources are doctors, special education teachers, and mental health professionals who can help identify learning disabilities and recommend the right combination of medical, psychosocial, and educational treatment.

You'll also read the stories of Susan, Wallace, and Dennis, three people who have learning disabilities. Although each had a rough start, with help they learned to cope with their handicaps. You'll see their early frustrations, their steps toward getting help, and their hopes for the future.

The stories of Susan, Wallace, and Dennis are representative of people with learning disabilities, but the characters are not real. Of course, people with learning disabilities are not all alike, so these stories may not fit any particular individual.

Understanding The Problem:
Susan

At age 14, Susan still tends to be quiet. Ever since she was a child, she was so withdrawn that people sometimes forgot she was there. She seemed to drift into a world of her own. When she did talk, she often called objects by the wrong names. She had few friends and mostly played with dolls or her little sister. In school, Susan hated reading and math because none of the letters, numbers or "plus" and "negative" signs made any sense. She felt awful about herself, She'd been told — and was convinced — that she was retarded.

Wallace

Wallace has lived 46 years, and still has trouble understanding what people say. Even as a boy, many words sounded alike, His father patiently said things over and over. But whenever his mother was drunk, she flew into a rage and spanked him for not listening. Wallace's speech also came out funny. He had such problems saying words that in school his teacher sometimes couldn't understand him. When classmates called him a "dummy", his fists just seemed to take over.

Dennis

Dennis is 23 years old and still seems to have too much energy. But he had always been an overactive boy, sometimes jumping on the sofa for hours until he collapsed with exhaustion. In grade school, he never sat still. He interrupted lessons.

But he was a friendly, well-meaning kid, so adults didn't get too angry. His academic problems became evident in third grade, when his teacher realized that Dennis could only recognize a few words and wrote like a first grader. She recommended that Dennis repeat third grade, to give him time to "catch-up." After another full year, his behavior was still out of control, and his reading and writing had not improved.

What Is A Learning Disability?

Unlike other disabilities, such as paralysis or blindness, a learning disability (LD) is a hidden handicap. A learning disability doesn't disfigure or leave visible signs that would invite others to be understanding or offer support. A woman once blurted to Wallace, "You seem so intelligent — you don't look handicapped!"

LD is a disorder that affects people's ability to either interpret what they see and hear or to link information from different parts of the brain. These limitations can show up in many ways — as specific difficulties with spoken and written language, coordination, self-control, or attention. Such difficulties extend to schoolwork and can impede learning to read or write, or to do math.

Learning disabilities can be lifelong conditions that, in some cases, affect many parts of a person's life, and sometimes even friendships and play. In some people, many overlapping learning disabilities may be apparent. Other people may have a single, isolated learning problem that has little impact on other areas of their lives.

What Are The Types Of Learning Disabilities?

"Learning disability" is not a diagnosis in the same sense as "chickenpox" or "mumps" Chickenpox and mumps imply a single, known cause with a predictable set of symptoms. Rather, LD is a broad term that covers a pool of possible causes, symptoms, treatments, and outcomes. Partly because learning disabilities can show up in so many forms, it is difficult to diagnose or to pinpoint the causes. And no one knows of a pill or remedy that will cure them.

Not all learning problems are necessarily learning disabilities. Many children are simply slower in developing certain skills. Because children show natural differences in their rate of development, sometimes what seems to be a learning disability may simply be a delay in maturation. To be diagnosed as a learning disability, specific criteria must be met.

The criteria and characteristics for diagnosing learning disabilities appear in a reference book called the DSM (short for the Diagnostic and Statistical Manual Disorder). The DSM diagnosis is commonly used when applying for health insurance coverage of diagnostic and treatment services.

Learning disabilities Can Be Divided Into Three Broad Categories:

1. Developmental speech and language disorders.

2. Academic skills disorders.

3. "Other," a catch-all that includes certain coordination disorders and learning handicaps not covered by the other terms.

Each of these categories includes a number of more specific disorders.

Developmental Speech And Language Disorder:

Speech and language problems are often the earliest indicators of a learning disability. People with developmental speech and language disorders have difficulty producing speech sounds, using spoken language to communicate, or understanding what others say.

Depending On The Problem, Specific Diagnosis May Be:

1. Developmental articulation disorder.

2. Developmental expressive language disorder.

3. Developmental receptive language disorder.

Developmental Articulation Disorder:

Children with this disorder may have trouble controlling their rate of speech. Or they may lag behind playmates in learning to make speech sounds. For example, Wallace at age 6 still said "wabbit" instead of "rabbit" and "thwim" for "swim." Developmental articulation disorders are common. They appear in at least 10 percent of children younger than age 8. Fortunately, articulation disorders can often be outgrown or successfully treated with speech therapy.

Developmental Expressive Language Disorder:

Some children with language impairments have problems expressing themselves in speech. Their disorder is called a developmental expressive language disorder. Susan, who often calls objects by the wrong names, has an expressive language disorder. Of course, an expressive language disorder can take other forms. A 4-year-old who speaks only in two-word phrases and a 6 year-old that can't answer simple questions also have an expressive language disability.

Developmental Receptive Language Disorder:

Some people have trouble understanding certain aspects of speech. It's as if their brains are set to a different frequency and the reception is poor. There's the toddler who doesn't respond to his name, a preschooler who hands you a bell when you ask for a ball, or the worker who consistently can't follow simple directions. Their hearing is fine, but they can't make sense of certain sounds, words, or sentences they hear. They may even seem inattentive. These people have a receptive language disorder. Because using and understanding speech are strongly related, many people with receptive language disorders also have an expressive language disability,

Of course in preschoolers, some misuse of sounds, words, or grammar is a normal part of learning to speak. It's only when these problems persist that there is any cause for concern.

Academic Skills Disorders:

Students with academic skills disorders are often years behind their classmates in developing reading, writing, or arithmetic skills.

The Diagnoses In This Category Include:

1.   Developmental reading disorder.
2.   Developmental writing disorder.
3.   Developmental arithmetic disorder.

Developmental Reading Disorder:

This type of disorder, also known as dyslexia, is quite widespread. In fact, reading disabilities affect 2 to 8 percent of elementary school children. When you think of what is involved in the "three R's" — reading, 'riting, and 'rithmetic — it's astounding that most of us do learn them.

Consider That To Read, You Must Simultaneously:

1. Focus attention on the printed marks and control eye movements across the page.

2. Recognize the sounds associated with letters.

3. Understanding words and grammar.

4. Build ideas and images.

5. Compare new ideas to what you already know.

6. Store ideas in memory.

Such mental juggling requires a rich, intact network of nerve cells that connect the brain's centers of vision, language, and memory.

A person can have problems in any of the tasks involved in reading. However, scientists found that a significant number of people with dyslexia share an inability to distinguish or separate the sounds in spoken words. Dennis, for example, can't identify the word "bat" by sounding out the individual letters, b-a-t. Other children with dyslexia may have trouble with rhyming games, such as rhyming. "cat" "bat". Yet scientists have found these skills fundamental to learning to read. Fortunately, remedial reading specialist have developed techniques that can help many children with dyslexia acquire these skills.

However, there is more to reading than recognizing words. If the brain is unable to form images or relate new ideas to those stored   in memory, the reader can't understand or remember the new concepts. So other types of reading disabilities can appear in the upper grades when the focus of reading shifts from word identification to comprehension.

Developmental Writing Disorder:

Writing too, involves several brain areas and functions. The brain networks for vocabulary, grammar, hand movement, and memory must all be in good working order. So a developmental writing disorder may result from problems in any of these areas, For example, Dennis, who was unable to distinguish the sequence of sounds in a word, had problems with spelling. A child with a writing disability, particularly an expressive language disorder, might be unable to compose complete, grammatical sentences.

Developmental Arithmetic Disorder:

If you doubt that arithmetic is a complex process, think of the steps you take to solve this simple problem: $25 \div 3 = ?$

Arithmetic involves recognizing numbers and symbols, memorizing facts such as the multiplication table, aligning numbers, and understanding abstract concepts like place value and fractions. Any of these may be difficult for children with developmental arithmetic disorders. Problems with numbers or basic concepts are likely to show up early. Disabilities that appear in the later grades are more often tied to problems in reasoning.

Many aspects, of speaking, listening, reading, writing, and arithmetic overlap and build on the same brain capabilities. So it's not surprising that people can be diagnosed as having more than one area of learning disability. For example, the ability to understand language underlines learning to speak. Therefore, any disorder that hinders the ability to understand language will also interfere with the development of speech, which in turn hinders learning to read and write. A single gap in the brain's operation can disrupt many types of activity.

"Other" Learning Disabilities:

The DSM also lists additional categories, such as "motor skills disorders" and "specific developmental disorders not otherwise specified." These diagnoses include delays in acquiring language, academic, and motor skills that can affect the ability to learn, but do not meet the criteria for a specific learning disability. Also included are coordination disorders that can lead to poor penmanship, as well as certain spelling and memory disorders.

Attention Disorders:

Nearly 4 million school-age children have learning disabilities. Of these, at least 20, percent have a type of disorder that leaves them unable to focus their attention.

Some children and adults who have attention disorders appear to daydream excessively. And once you get their attention, they're often easily distracted. Susan, for example, tends to mentally drift off into a world of her own. Children like Susan may have a number of learning difficulties. If, like Susan, they are quiet and don't cause problems, their problems may go unnoticed. They may be passed along from grade to grade, without getting the special assistance they need,

In a large proportion of affected children — mostly boys — the attention deficit is accompanied by hyperactivity. Dennis is an example of a person with attention deficit hyperactivity disorder — ADHD. Like young Dennis, who jumped on the sofa to exhaustion, hyperactive children can't sit still. They act impulsively, running into traffic or toppling desks. They blurt out answers and interrupt. In games, they can't wait their turn. These children's problems are usually hard to miss. Because of their constant motion and explosive energy, hyperactive children often get into trouble with parents, teachers, and peers.

By adolescence, physical hyperactivity usually subsides into fidgeting and restlessness. But the problems with attention and concentration often continue into adulthood. At work, adults with ADHD often have trouble organizing tasks or completing their work. They don't seem to listen to or follow directions. Their work may be messy and appear careless,

Attention disorders, with or without hyperactivity, are not considered learning disabilities in themselves. However, because attention problems can seriously interfere with school performance, they often accompany academic skills disorders.

What Causes Learning Disabilities?

Understandably, one of the first questions parents ask when they learn their child has a learning disorder is "Why? What went wrong?"

Mental health professionals stress that since no one knows what causes learning disabilities, it doesn't help parents to, look backward to search for possible reasons. There are too many possibilities to pin down the cause. The family must move forward to get the right help.

Scientists, however, do need to study causes in an effort to identify ways to prevent learning disabilities.

Once, scientists thought that all learning disabilities were caused by a single neurological problem. But research support by NIMH has helped us see that the causes are more diverse and complex. New evidence seems to show that most learning disabilities do not stem from a single, specific area of the brain, but from difficulties in bringing together information from its different regions.

Today, a leading theory is that learning disabilities stem from subtle disturbances in brain structures and functions. Some scientists believe that, in many cases, the disturbance begins before birth.

Errors In Fetal Brain Development:

Throughout pregnancy, the fetal brain develops from a few all-purpose cells into a complex organ made of billions of specialized, interconnected nerve cells called neurons. During this amazing evolution, things can go wrong that may alter how the neurons form or interconnect.

In the early stages of pregnancy, the brain stem forms. It controls basic life functions such as breathing and digestion. Later, a deep ridge divides the cerebrum — the thinking part of the brain — into two halves, a right and left hemisphere. Finally, the areas involved with processing sight, sound, and other senses develop, as well as the areas associated with attention, thinking, and emotion.

As new cells form, they move into place to create various brain structures. Nerve cells rapidly grow to form networks with other parts of the brain. These networks are what allow information to be shared among various regions of the brain.

Throughout pregnancy, this brain development is vulnerable to disruptions. If the disruption occurs early, the fetus may   die, or the infant may be born with widespread disabilities and possibly mental retardation. If the disruption occurs later, when the cells are becoming specialized and moving into place, it may leave errors in the cell makeup, location, or connections. Some scientists believe that these errors may later show up as learning disorders.

Other Factors That Affect Brain Development:

Through experiments with animals, scientists at NIMH and other research facilities are tracking clues to determine what disrupts brain development. By studying the normal process of brain development, scientists can better understand what can go wrong. Some of these studies are examining how genes, substance abuse, pregnancy problems, and toxins may affect the developing brain.

Genetic Factors:

The fact that learning disabilities tend to run in families indicates that there may be a genetic link. For example, children who lack some of the skills needed for reading, such as hearing the separate sounds of words, are likely to have a parent with a related problem. However, a parent's learning disability may take a slightly different form in the child. A parent who has a writing disorder may have a child with an expressive language disorder. For this reason, it seems unlikely that specific learning disorders are inherited directly. Possibly, what is inherited is a subtle brain dysfunction that can in turn lead to a learning disability.

There may be an alternative explanation for why LD might seem to run in families. Some learning difficulties may actually stem from the family environment. For example, parents who have expressive language disorders might talk less to their children, or the language they use may be distorted. In such cases, the child lacks a good model for acquiring language and therefore, may seem to be learning disabled.

Tobacco, Alcohol, And Other Drug Use:

Many drugs taken by the mother pass directly to the fetus. Research shows that a mother's use of cigarettes, alcohol, or other drugs during pregnancy may have damaging effects on the unborn child. Therefore, to prevent potential harm to developing babies, the U.S. Public Health Service supports efforts to make people aware of the possible dangers of smoking, drinking, and using drugs,

Scientists have found that mothers who smoke during pregnancy may be more likely to bear smaller babies. This is a concern because small newborns, usually those weighing less than 5 pounds, tend to be a risk for a variety of problems, including learning disorders.

Alcohol also may be dangerous to the fetus' developing brain. It appears that alcohol may distort the developing neurons. Heavy alcohol use during pregnancy has been linked to fetal alcohol syndrome, a condition that can lead to low birth weight, intellectual impairment, hyperactivity, and certain physical defects. Any alcohol use during pregnancy, however, may influence the child's development and lead to problems with learning, attention, memory, or problem solving. Because scientists have not yet identified "safe" levels, alcohol should be used cautiously by women who are pregnant.

Drugs such as cocaine — especially in its smokable form known as crack — seem to affect the normal development of brain receptors. These brain cell parts help to transmit incoming signals from our skin, eyes, and ears, and help regulate out physical response to the environment. Because children with certain learning disabilities have difficulty understanding speech sounds or letters, some researchers believe that learning disabilities, as well as ADHD, may be related to faulty receptors. Current research points to drug abuse as a possible cause of receptor damage.

Problems During Pregnancy Or Delivery:

Other possible causes of learning disabilities involve complications during pregnancy. In some cases, the mother's immune system reacts to the fetus and attacks it as if it were an infection. This type of disruption seems to cause newly formed brain cells to settle in the wrong part of the brain. Or during delivery, the umbilical cord may become twisted and temporarily cut off oxygen to the fetus. This, too, can impair brain functions and lead to LD.

Toxins In The Child's Environment:

New brain cells and neural networks continue to be produced for a year or so after the child is born. These cells are vulnerable to certain disruptions, also.

Researchers are looking into environmental toxins that may lead to learning disabilities, possibly by disrupting childhood brain development or brain processes. Cadmium and lead, both prevalent in the environment, are becoming a leading focus of neurological research. Cadmium, used in making some steel products, can get into the soil, then into the foods we eat. Lead was once common in paint and gasoline, and is still present in some water pipes. A study of animals sponsored by the National Institutes of Health showed a connection between exposure to lead and learning difficulties. In the study, rats exposed to lead experienced changes in their brainwaves, slowing their ability to learn. The learning problems lasted for weeks, long after the rats were no longer exposed to lead.

In addition, there is growing evidence that learning problems may develop in children with cancer who had been treated with chemotherapy or radiation at an early age. This seems particularly true of children with brain tumors who received radiation to the skull.

Are Learning Disabilities Related To Differences In The Brain?

In comparing people with and without learning disabilities, scientists have observed certain differences in the structure and functioning of the brain. For example, new research indicates that there may be variations in the brain structure called the planum temporale, a language-related area found in both sides of the brain. In people with dyslexia, the two structures were found to be equal in size. In people who are not dyslexic, however, the left planum temporale was noticeably larger. Some scientists believe reading problems may be related to such differences.

With more research, scientists hope to learn precisely how differences in the structures and processes of the brain contribute to learning disabilities, and how these differences might be treated or prevented.

A) Getting Help:
Susan

Susan was promoted to the six grade but still couldn't do basic math. So, her mother brought her to a private clinic for testing. The children observed that Susan had trouble associating symbols with their meaning, and this was holding back her language, reading, and math development. Susan called objects by the wrong words and she could not associate sounds with letters or recognize math symbols. However, an IQ of 126 meant that Susan was quite bright. In addition to developing an Individualized Education Plan, the clinician recommended that Susan receive counseling for her low self-esteem and depression.

Wallace

In the early 1960s, at the request of his ninth grade teacher, Wallace was examined by a doctor to see why he didn't speak or listen well. The doctor tested his vocal cords, vision, and hearing. They were all fine. The teacher concluded that Wallace must have "brain damage," so not much could be done. Wallace kept failing in school and was suspended several times for fighting. He finally dropped out after tenth grade. He spent the next 25 years working as a janitor. Because LD frequently went undiagnosed at the time when Wallace was young, the needed help was not available to him.

Dennis

In fifth grade, Dennis' teacher sent him to the school psychologist for testing. Dennis was diagnosed as having developmental reading and developmental writing disorder, He was also identified as having an attention disorder with hyperactivity. He was placed in an all-day special education program, where he could work on his particular deficits and get individual attention. His family doctor prescribed the medication Ritalin to reduce his hyperactivity and distractibility. Along with working to improve his reading, the special education teacher helped him improve his listening skills. Since his handwriting was still poor, he learned to type homework and reports on a computer. At age 19, Dennis graduated from high school and was accepted by a college that gives special assistance to students with learning disabilities.

How Are Learning Disabilities First Identified?

The first step in solving any problem is realizing there is one. Wallace, sadly, was a product of his time, when learning disabilities were more of a mystery and often went unrecognized. Today, professionals would know how to help Wallace. Dennis and Susan were able to get help because someone saw the problem and referred them for help,

When a baby is born, the parents eagerly wait for the baby's first step, first word, a myriad of other "firsts." During routine checkups, the pediatrician, too, watches for more subtle signs of development. The parents and doctor are watching for the child to achieve developmental milestones.

How Are Learning Disabilities Formally Diagnosed?

Parents are usually the first to notice obvious delays in their child reaching early milestones. The pediatrician may observe, more subtle signs of minor neurological damage, such as a lack of coordination. But the classroom teacher, in fact, may be the first to notice the child's persistent difficulties in reading, writing, or arithmetic. As school tasks become more complex, a child with a learning disability may have problems mentally juggling more information.

The learning problems of children who are quiet and polite in school may go unnoticed. Children with above average intelligence, who manage to maintain passing grades despite their disability, are even less likely to be identified. Children with hyperactivity, on the other hand, will be identified quickly by their impulsive behavior and excessive movement. Hyperactivity usually begins before age 4 but may not be recognized until the child enters school.

What should parents, doctors, and teachers do if critical developmental milestones haven't appeared by the usual age? Sometimes it's best to allow a little more time, simply for the brain to mature a bit. But if a milestone is already long delayed, if there's a history of learning disabilities in the family, or it there are several delayed skills, the child should be professionally evaluated as soon as possible. An educator or doctor who treats children can suggest where to go for help. By law, learning disability is defined as a significant gap between a person's intelligence and the skills the person has achieved at each age. This means that a severely retarded 10-year-old who speaks like a 6-year-old probably doesn't have a language or speech disability. He has mastered language up to the limits of his intelligence. On the other hand, a fifth grader with an IQ of a hundred who can't write a simple sentence probably does have LD.

Learning disorders may be informally flagged by observing significant delays in the child's skill development. A 2-year delay in the primary grades is usually considered significant, For older students, such a delay is not as debilitating, so learning disabilities aren't usually suspected unless there is more than a 2-year delay. Actual diagnosis of learning disabilities, however, is made using standardized tests that compare the child's level of ability to what is considered normal development for a person of that age and intelligence.

For example, as late as fifth grade, Susan couldn't add two numbers, even though she rarely missed school and was good in other subjects. Her mother took her to a clinician, which observed Susan's behavior and administered standardized math and intelligence tests. The test results showed that Susan's math skills were several years behind, given her mental capacity for learning. Once other possible causes like lack of motivation and vision problems were ruled out, Susan's math problem was formally diagnosed as a specific learning disability.

Test outcomes depend not only on the child's actual abilities, but on the reliability of the test and the child's ability to pay attention and understand the questions. Children like Dennis, with poor attention or hyperactivity, may score several points below their true level of ability. Testing a child in an isolated room can sometimes help the child concentrate and score higher.

Each type of LD is diagnosed in slightly different ways. To diagnose speech and language disorder, a speech therapist tests the child's pronunciation, vocabulary, and grammar and compares them to the developmental abilities seen in most children that age. A psychologist tests the child's intelligence. A physician checks for any ear infections, and an audiologist may be consulted to rule out auditory problems. If the problem involves articulation, a doctor examines the child's vocal cords and throat.

In the case of academic skills disorder, academic development in reading, writing, and math is evaluated using standardized tests. In addition, vision and hearing are tested to be sure the student can see words clearly and can hear adequately. The specialist also checks if the child has missed much school. It's important to rule out these possible factors. After all, treatment for a learning disability is very different from the remedy for poor vision or missing school.

ADHD is diagnosed by checking for the long-term presence of specific behaviors, such as considerable fidgeting, losing things, interrupting and talking excessively. Other signs include an inability to remain seated, stay on task, or take turns. A diagnosis of ADHD is made only if the child shows such behaviors substantially more than other children of the same age.

If the school fails to notice a learning delay, parents can request an outpatient evaluation. In Susan's case, her mother chose to bring Susan to a clinic for testing. She then brought documentation of the disability back to the school. After confirming the diagnosis, the public school was obligated to provide the kind of instructional program that Susan needed.

Parents should stay abreast of each step of the school's evaluation. Parents also need to know that they may appeal the school's decision if they disagree with the findings of the diagnostic team. And like Susan's mother, who brought Susan to a clinic, parents always have the option of getting a second opinion.

Some parents feel alone and confused when talking to learning specialists. Such parents may find it helpful to ask someone they like and trust to go with them to school meetings. The person may be the child's clinician or caseworker, or even a neighbor. It can help to have someone along who knows the child and can help understand the child's test scores or learning problem.

What Are The Education Options?

Although obtaining a diagnosis is important, even more important is creating a plan for getting the right help. Because LD can affect the child and family in so many ways, help may be needed on a variety of fronts: educational, medical, emotional, and practical.

In most ways, children with learning disabilities are no different from children without these disabilities. At school, they eat together and share sports, games, and after-school activities. But since children with learning disabilities do have specific learning needs, most public schools provide special programs.

Schools typically provide special education programs in a separate all-day classroom or as a special education class that the student attends for several hours each week. Some parents hire trained tutors to work with their child after school. If the problems are severe, some parents choose to place their child in a special school for the learning disabled.

If parents choose to get help outside the public schools, they should select a learning specialist carefully The specialist should be able to explain things in terms that the parents can understand. Whenever possible, the specialist should have professional certification and experience with the learner's specific age group and type of disability. Some of the support groups listed at the end of this section can provide references to qualified special education programs.

Planning a special education program begins with systematically identifying what the student can and cannot do. The specialist looks for patterns in the child's gaps. For example, if the child fails to hear the separate sounds in words, are there other sound discrimination problems? If there's a problem with handwriting, are there other motor delays? Are there any consistent problems with memory?

Special education teachers also identify the types of tasks the child can do and the senses that function well. By using the senses that are intact and bypassing the disabilities, many children can develop needed skills. These strengths offer alternative ways the child can learn.

After assessing the child's strengths and weaknesses, the special education teacher designs an Individualized Educational Program (IEP). The IEP outlines the specific skills the child needs to develop as well as appropriate learning activities that build on the child's strengths. Many effective learning activities engage several skills and senses. For example, in learning to spell and recognize words, a student may be asked to see, say, write, and spell each new word. The student may also write the words in sand, which engages the sense of touch. Many experts believe that the more senses children use in learning a skill, the more likely they are to retain it.

An individualized, skill-based approach — like the approach used by speech and language therapists — often succeeds in helping where regular classroom instruction fails. Therapy for speech and language disorders focuses on providing a stimulating but structured environment for hearing and practicing language patterns. For example, the therapist may help a child who has an articulation disorder to produce specific speech sounds. During an engaging activity, the therapist may talk about the toys, then encourage the child to use same sounds or words. In addition, the child may watch the therapist's throat, then practice making the sounds before a mirror.

Researchers are also investigating non-standard teaching methods. Some create artificial learning conditions that may help the brain receive information in non-standard ways. For example, in some language disorders, the brain seems abnormally slow to process verbal information. Scientists are testing whether computers that talk can help teach children to process spoken sounds more quickly. The computer starts slowly, pronouncing one sound at a time. As the child gets better at recognizing the sounds and hearing them as words, the sounds are gradually speeded up to a normal rate of speech.

Is Medication Available?

For nearly six decades, many children with attention disorders have benefited from being treated with medication. Three drugs, Ritalin (methylphenidate), Dexedrine (dextroamphetamine), and Cylert (pemoline), have been used successfully. Although these drugs are stimulants in the same category as "speed" and "diet pills," they seldom make children "high" or more, jittery. Rather, they temporarily improve children's attention and ability to focus. They also help children control their impulsiveness other hyperactive behaviors.

The effects of medication are most dramatic in children with ADHD. Shortly after taking the medication, they become more able to focus their attention. They become more ready to learn. Studies by NIMH scientist and other researchers have shown that at least 90% of hyperactive children can be helped by either Ritalin or Dexedrine. If one medication does not help a hyperactive child to calm down and pay-attention in school, the other medication might.

The drugs are effective for 3 to 4 hours and move out of the body within 12 hours. The child's doctor or a psychiatrist works closely with the family and child to carefully adjust the dosage and medication schedule for the best effect. Typically, the child takes the medication so that the drug is active during peak school hours, such as when reading, and math are taught.

In the past few years, researchers have tested these drugs on adults who have attention disorders. Just as in children, the results show that low doses of these medications can help reduce distractibility and impulsivity in adults. Use of these medications has made it possible for many severely disordered adults to organize their lives, hold jobs, and care for themselves.

In trying to do everything possible to help their children many, parents have been quick to try new treatments. Most of these treatments sound scientific and reasonable, but a few are pure quackery. Many are developed by reputable doctors or specialists — but when tested scientifically, cannot be proven to help.

Following Are Types Of Therapy That Have Not Proven Effective In Treating The Majority Of Children With Learning Disabilities Or Attention Disorders:

1.   Megavitamins.

2.   Colored lenses.

3.   Special diets.

4.   Sugar-free diets.

5.   Body stimulation or manipulation.

Although scientists hope that brain research will lead to new medical interventions and drugs, at present there are no medicines for speech, language, or academic disabilities.

How Do Families Learn To Cope?

The effects of learning disabilities can ripple outward from, the disabled child or adult to family, friends, and peers at school or work.

Children with LD often absorb what others thoughtlessly say about them. They may define themselves in light of their disabilities, as "behind," "slow," or "different."

Sometimes they don't know how they're different, but they know how awful they feel. Their tension or shame can lead them to act out in various ways — from withdrawal to belligerence. Like Wallace, they may get into fights. They may stop trying to learn and achieve and eventually drop out of school. Or, like Susan, they may become isolated and depressed.

Children with learning disabilities and attention disorders may have trouble making friends with peers. For children with ADHD, this may be due to their impulsive, hostile, or withdrawn behavior. Some children with delays may be more comfortable with younger children who play at their level. Social problems may also be a product of their disability. Some people with LD seem unable to interpret tone of voice or facial expressions Misunderstanding the situation, they act inappropriately turning people away.

Without professional help, the situation can spiral out of control. The more that children or teenagers fail, the more they may act out their frustration and damage their self-esteem, The more they act out, the more trouble and punishment it brings, further lowering their self-esteem. Wallace, who lashed out when teased about his poor pronunciation and was repeatedly suspended from school, shows how harmful this cycle can be.

Having a child with a learning disability may also be an emotional burden for the family. Parents often sweep through a range of emotions: denial, guilt, blame, frustration, anger, and despair. Brothers and sisters may be annoyed or embarrassed by their sibling, or jealous of all the attention the child with LD gets.

Counseling can be very helpful to people with LD and their families. Counseling can help affected children, teenagers, and adults develop greater self-control and a more positive attitude toward their own abilities. Talking with a counselor or psychologist also allows family members to air their feelings as well as get support and reassurance.

Many parents find that joining a support group also makes a difference. Support groups can be a source of information, practical suggestions, and mutual understanding. Self-help books written by educators and mental health professionals can also be helpful. A number of references and support groups are listed at the end of this section.

Behavior modification also seems to help many children with hyperactivity and LD. In behavior modification, children receive immediate, tangible rewards when they act appropriately. Receiving an immediate reward can help children learn to control their own actions, both at home and in class. A school or private counselor can explain behavior modification and help parents and teachers set up appropriate rewards for the child.

Parents and teachers can help by structuring tasks and environments for the in ways that allow the child to succeed. They can find ways to help children build on their strengths and work around their disabilities. This may mean deliberately making eye contact before speaking to a child with an attention disorder. For teenagers with a language problem, it may mean providing pictures and diagrams for performing a task. For students like Dennis with handwriting or spelling problems, a solution may be to provide a word processor and software that checks spelling. A counselor or school psychologist can help identify practical solutions that make it easier for the child and family to cope day by day.

Every child needs to grow up feeling competent and loved. When children have learning disabilities, parents may need to work harder at developing their children's self-esteem and relationship-building skills. But self-esteem and good relationships are as worth developing as any academic skill.

B) Sustaining Hope:
Susan

Susan is now in the ninth grade and enjoys learning. She no longer believes she's retarded, and her use of words has improved. Susan has become a talented craftsperson and. loves making clothes and furniture for her sister's dolls. Although she's still in a special education programs, she is making slow but steady progress in reading and math.

Wallace

Over the years, Wallace found he liked tinkering with cars and singing in the church choir. At church he meet a woman who knew about learning disabilities. She told him he could get help through his county social services. Since then, Wallace has been working with a speech therapist, learning to articulate and notice differences in speech sounds. When he complains that he's too old to learn, his therapist reminds him, "It's never too late to work your good brain!" His state vocational rehabilitation office recently referred him to a job-training program. Today, at age 46, Wallace is starting night school to become an auto mechanic. He likes it because it's a hands-on program where he can learn by doing.

Dennis

Dennis is now age 23. As he walks into the college job placement office, he smiles and shakes hands confidently. After shuffling through a messy stack of papers, he finally hands his counselor a neatly typed resume. Although Dennis jiggles his foot and interrupts occasionally, he's clearly enthusiastic. He explains that because tape-recorded books and lectures got him through college, he'd like to sell electronics. Dennis says he'll also be getting married next year. He and his fiancée are concerned that their children also will have LD. "But we'll just have to watch and get help early — a lot earlier than I did!"

Can Learning Disabilities Be Outgrown Or Cured?

Even through most people don't out grow their brain dysfunction, people do learn to adapt and live fulfilling lives. Dennis, Susan, and Wallace made a life for themselves — not by being cured but by developing their personal strengths. Like Dennis' tape-recorded books and lectures, or Wallace's hands-on auto mechanics class, they found alternative ways to learn. And like Susan's crafts or Wallace's singing, they found ways to enjoy their other talents.

Even though a learning disability doesn't disappear, given the right types of educational experiences, people have a remarkable ability to learn. The brain's flexibility to learn new skills is probably greatest in young children and may diminish somewhat after puberty. This is why early intervention is so important. Nevertheless, we retain the ability to learn throughout our lives.

Even though learning disabilities can't be cured, there is still cause for hope. Because certain learning problems reflect delayed development, many children do eventually catch up. Of the speech and language disorders, children who have an articulation or an expressive language disorder are the least likely to have long-term problems. Despite initial delays, most children do learn to speak.

For people with dyslexia, the outlook is mixed. But an appropriate remedial reading program can help learners make great strides.

With age, and appropriate help from parents and clinicians, children with ADHD become better able to suppress their hyperactivity and to channel it into more socially acceptable behaviors. As with Dennis, the problem may take less disruptive forms, such as fidgeting.

Can an adult be helped? For example, can an adult with dyslexia still learn to read? In many cases, the answer is yes. It may not come as easily as for a child. It may take more time and more repetition, and it may even take more diverse teaching methods. But we know more about reading and about adult learning than ever before. We know that adults have a wealth of life experience to build on as they learn. And because adults choose to learn, they do so with a determination that most children don't have. A variety of literacy and adult education programs sponsored by libraries, public schools, and community colleges are available to help adults develop skills in reading, writing, and math. Some of these programs, as well as private and nonprofit tutoring and learning centers, provide appropriate programs for adults with LD.

What Aid Does The Government Offer?

As of 1981, people with learning disabilities came under the protection of the laws originally designed to protect the rights of people with mobility handicaps. more recent Federal laws specifically guarantee equal opportunity and raise the level of services to people with disabilities. Once a learning disability is identified, children are guaranteed a free public education specifically designed around their individual needs. Adolescents with disabilities can receive practical assistance and extra training to help make the transition to jobs and independent living. Adults have access to job training and technology that open new doors of opportunity.

Increased Services, Equal Opportunity:

The Individuals with Disabilities Education Act of 1990 assures a public education to school-aged children with diagnosed learning disabilities. Under this act, public schools are required to design and implement an Individualized Educational Program tailored to each child's specific needs. The 1991 Individuals with Disabilities Education Act extended services to developmentally delayed children down to age 5. This law makes it possible for young children to receive help even before they begin school.

Another law, the Americans with Disabilities Act of 1990 guarantees equal employment opportunity for people with learning disabilities and protects disabled workers against job discrimination. Employers may not consider the learning disability when selecting among job applicants. Employers must also make "reasonable accommodations" to help workers who have handicaps do their job. Such accommodations may include shifting job responsibilities, modifying equipment, or adjusting work schedules.

By law, publicly funded colleges and universities must also remove barriers that keep out disabled students. As a result, many colleges now recruit and work with students with learning disabilities to make it possible for them to attend. Depending on the student's areas of difficulty, this help may include providing recorded books and lectures, providing an isolated area to take tests, or allowing a student to tape record rather than write reports. Students with learning disabilities can arrange to take college entrance exams orally or in isolated rooms free from distraction. Many colleges are creating special programs to specifically accommodate these students.

Programs like these made it possible for Dennis to attend and succeed in college. The HEATH Resource Center, sponsored by the American Council on Education, assists students with learning disabilities to identify appropriate colleges and universities. Information on the HEATH center and related organizations appears at the end of this section.

Public Agency Support:

Effective service agencies are also in place to assist people of all ages. Each state department of education can help parents identify the requirements and the process for getting special education services for their child. Other agencies serve disabled infants and preschool children. Still others offer mental health and counseling services. The Nation Information Center for Children and Youth can provide referrals to appropriate local resources and state agencies.

Counselors at each state department of vocational rehabilitation serve the employment needs of adolescents and adults with learning disabilities. They can refer adults to free or subsidized health care, counseling, and high school equivalence (GED) programs. They can assist in arranging for job training that sidesteps the disability. For example, a vocational counselor helped Wallace identify his aptitude for car repair. To work around Wallace's language problems, the counselor helped located a job-training program that teaches through demonstrations and active practice rather than lectures.

State departments of vocational rehabilitation can also assist in finding special equipment that can make it possible for disabled individuals to receive training, retain a job, or live on their own. For example, because Dennis couldn't read the electronics manuals in his new job, a vocational rehabilitation counselor helped him locate and purchase a special computer that reads books aloud.

Finally, state-run protection and advocacy agencies and client assistance programs serve to protect these rights. As experts on the laws, they offer legal assistance as well as information about local health, housing, and social services.

What Hope Does Research Offer?

Sophisticated brain imaging technology is now making it possible to directly observe the brain at work and to detect subtle malfunctions that could never be seen before. Other techniques allow scientists to study the points of contact among brain cells and the ways signals are transmitted from cell to cell.

With this array of technology, NIMH is conducting research to identify which parts of the brain are used during certain activities, such as reading. For example, researchers are comparing the brain processes of people with and without dyslexia as they read. Research of this kind may eventually associate portions of the brain with different reading problems.

Clinical research also continues to amass data on the causes of learning disorders. NIMH grantees at Yale are examining the brain structures of children with different combinations of learning disabilities. Such research will help identify differences in the nervous system of children with these related disorders. Eventually, scientists will know, for example, whether children who have both dyslexia and an attention disorder will benefit from the same treatment as dyslexic children without an attention disorder.

Studies of identical and fraternal twins are also being conducted. Identical twins have the same genetic makeup, while fraternal twins do not. By studying if learning disabilities are more likely to be shared by identical twins than fraternal twins, researchers hope to determine whether these disorders are influenced more by genetic or by environmental factors. One such study is being conducted by scientist funded by the National Institute of Child Health and Human Development. So far, research indicates that genes may, in fact, influence the ability to sound out words.

Animal studies also are adding to our knowledge of learning disabilities in humans. Animal subjects make it possible to study some of the possible causes of LD in ways that can't be studied in humans. One NIMH grantee is researching the effects of barbiturates and other drugs that are sometimes prescribed during pregnancy. Another researcher discovered through animal studies that certain prenatal viruses can affect future learning. Research of this kind may someday pinpoint prenatal problems that can trigger specific disabilities and tell us how they can be prevented.

Animal research also allows the safety and effectiveness of experimental new drugs to be tested long before they can be tried on humans. One NIMH-sponsored team is studying dogs to learn how new stimulant drugs that are similar to Ritalin act on the brain. Another is using mice to test a chemical that may counter memory loss.

This accumulation of data sets the stage for applied research. In the coming years, NIMH-sponsored research will focus on identifying the conditions that are required for learning and the best combination approaches for each child.

Piece by piece, using a myriad of research techniques and technologies, scientists are beginning to solve the puzzle. As research deepens our understanding, we approach a future where we can prevent certain brain and mental disorders, make valid diagnoses, and treat each effectively. This is the hope, mission, and vision of the National Institute of Mental Health.

What Are Sources Of Information And Support?

Several publications, organizations, and support groups exist to help individuals, teachers, and families to understand and cope with learning disabilities. The following resources provide a good starting point for gaining insight, practical solutions, and support. Further information can be found at libraries and bookstores.

Publications:
Books For Children And Teens With Learning Disabilities:

Fisher, G., and Cummings, R. The Survival Guide for Kids with LD. Minneapolis: Free Spirit Publishing, 1990. (Also available on cassette)

Gehret, J., Learning Disabilities and the Don't-Give-Up-Kid. Fairport, NY: Verbal Images Press, 1990.

Janover, C. Josh. A Boy with Dyslexia. Burlington, VT: Waterfront Books, 1988.

Landau, E. Dyslexia. New York: Franklin Watts Publishing Co., 1991

Marek, M. Different, Not Dumb. New York: Franklin Watts Publishing Co., 1985.

Levine, M. Keeping A Head in School: A Student's Book About Learning Abilities and Learning Disorders. Cambridge, MA: Educators Publishing Services, Inc., 1990.

Books For Adults With Learning Disabilities:

Adelman, P., and Wren, C. Learning Disabilities, Graduate School, and Careers: The Student's Perspective. Lake Forest, IL: Learning Opportunities Program, Barat College, 1990.

Cardoni, B. Living with a Learning Disability. Carbondale IL: Southern Illinois University Press, 1987.

Kravets, K. and Wax, I. The K&W Guide: Colleges and the Learning Disabled Student. New York: Harper Collins Publishers, 1992.

Magnum, C, and Strichard, S., eds. Colleges with Programs for Students with Learning Disabilities. Princeton, NJ: Petersons Guides, 1992.

Books For Parents:

Greene, L. Learning Disabilities and Your Child: A Survival Handbook. New York: Fawcett Columbine, 1987.

Novick, B., and Arnold, M. Why Is My Child Having Trouble in School? New York: Villard Books, 1991.

Silver. L. The Misunderstood Child: A Guide for Parents of Children with Learning Disabilities. 2d ed. Blue Ridge Summit, PA: Tab Books, 1992.

Silver, L. Dr. Silver's Advice to Parents on Attention-Deficit Hyperactivity Disorder. Washington, DC: American Psychiatric Press 1993.

Vail, P. Smart Kids With School Problems. New York: EP Dutton, 1987.

Weiss, E. Mothers Talk About Learning Disabilities. New York: Prentice Hall Press,

1989.
Books And Pamphlets For Teachers And Specialists:

Adelman, P., and Wren, C. Learning Disabilities, Graduate School, and Careers. Lake Forest, Learning Opportunities Program, Barat College, 1990.

Siver, L. ADHD: Attention Deficit-Hyperactivity Disorder, Booklet for Teachers. Summit NJ: CIBA-GEIGY, 1989.

Smith, S. Success Against the Odds: Strategies and Insights from the Learning Disabled. Los Angeles: Jeremy Tarcher, Inc., 1991.

Wender, P. The Hyperactive Child, Adolescent, and Adult. Attention Disorder through the Lifespan. New York: Oxford University Press, 1987.

Related Pamphlets Available From NIH:

Facts About Dyslexia
Nation Institute of Child Health and Human Development
Building 31, Room 2A32
9000 Rockville Pike
Bethesda, MD 20892
(301) 496-5133

Developmental Speech and Language Disorders — Hope through Research
National Institute on Deafness and Other Communicative Disorders
P.O. Box 37777
Washington, DC 20013
(800) 241-1044

Support Groups And Organizations:

American Speech-Language-Hearing Association
10301 Rockville Pike
Rockville, MD 20852,
(800) 638-8255
Provides information on speech and language disorders, as well as referrals to certified speech language therapists.

Attention Deficit Information Network
475 Hillside Avenue
Needham, MA 02194
 (617) 455-9895
Provides up-to-date information on current research, regional meetings. Offers aid in finding solutions to practical problems faced by adults and children with an attention disorder.

Candlelighters Childhood Cancer Foundation
1910 Woodmont Avenue, Suite 460
Bethesda, MD 20814
(900) 366-2223
Provides information and support for children treated for cancer who later experi-

ence learning disabilities.

Center for Mental Health Services
Office Of Consumer, Family, and Public Information
5600 Fisher Lane, Room 15-81
Rockville, MD 20857
(301) 443-2792
This new national center, a component of the U.S. Public Health Service, provides a range of information on mental health, treatment, and support services.

Children with Attention Deficit Disorders (CHADD)
499 NW 70th Avenue, Suite 308
Plantation, FL 33317
(305) 587-3700
Runs support groups and publishes two newsletters concerning attention disorders for parents and professionals.

Council for Exceptional Children
11920 Association Drive
Reston, VA 22091
(703) 620-3660
Provides publications for educators. Can also provide referral to ERIC Clearinghouse for Handicapped and Gifted Children.

Federation of Families for Children's Mental Health
1021 Prince Street
Alexandria, VA 22314
(703) 634-7710
Provides information support, and referrals through federation chapters throughout the country. This national parent-run organization focuses on the needs of children with broad mental health problems.

Health Resource Center
American Council on Education
1 Dupont Circle, Suite 800
Washington, DC 20036
(800) 544-3284
A national clearinghouse on post-high school education for people with disabilities.

Learning Disabilities Association of America
4156 Library Road
Pittsburgh, PA 15234
(412) 341-8077
Provides information and referrals to state chapters, parent resources, and local support groups. Publishes news briefs and a professional journal.

Library of Congress
National Library Service for the Blind and Physically Handicapped
1291 Taylor Street, NW
Washington, DC 20542 (202) 707-5100
Publishes Talking Books and Reading Disabilities, a factsheet outlines eligibility requirements for borrowing talking books.

National Alliance for the Mentally III
Children and Adolescents Network (NAMI CAN)
2101 Wilson Boulevard, Suite 302
Arlington. VA 22201
(800) 950-NAMI
Provides support to families through personal contact and support meetings. Provides education regarding coping strategies; reading material; and information about what works — and what doesn't.

Nation Association of Private Schools for Exceptional Children
1522 K Street, NW Suite 1032
Washington, DC 20005
Provides referrals to private special education programs.

National Center for Learning Disabilities
381 Park Avenue South, Suite 1420
New York, NY 10016
(212) 687-7211
Provides referrals and resources, "Their World" magazine describing true stories on ways children and adults cope with LD.

National Information Center for Children and Youth with Disabilities
P.O. Box 1492
Washington, DC 20013
(800) 999-5599
Publishes newsletters, arranges workshops. Advises parents on the laws entitling children with disabilities to special education and other services.

Orton Dyslexia Society
Chester Building, Suite 382
8600 LaSalle Road
Baltimore, MD 21286-2044
(410) 296-0232
Answers questions on reading disability. Provides information and referrals to local resources.

To arrange for special college entrance testing for LD adults, Contact:
ACT Special Testing (319) 337-1332
SAT Scholastic Aptitude Test (609) 939-9490
GED (202) 939-9490

Research conducted and supported by the National Institute of Mental Health brings hope to millions of people who suffer from mental illness and to their families and friends. In many years of work with animals as well as human subjects, researchers have advanced our understanding of the brain and vastly expanded the capability of mental health professionals to diagnose, treat, and prevent mental and brain disorders.

Now, in the 1990s, which the president and Congress have declared the "Decade of the Brain," we stand at the threshold of a new era in brain and behavior science.

Through research, we will learn even more about mental and brain disorders such as depression, bipolar disorder, schizophrenia, panic disorder, obsessive-compulsive disorder, and learning disabilities. And we will be able to use this knowledge to develop new therapies that can help more people overcome mental illness.

The National Institute of Mental Health is part of the National Institutes of Health (NIH), the Federal Government's primary agency for biomedical and behavioral research. NIH is a component of the U.S. Department of Health and Human Services.

Part 5
Helping Your Child Learn Responsible Behavior

Introduction

Our children deserve to learn important lessons from us and to acquire important habits with our help. They need help in learning what matters to us. We want our children to grow up to be responsible adults. We want them to learn to feel, think, and act with respect for themselves and for other people. We want them to pursue their own well-being, while also being considerate of the needs and feelings of others.

Today, there is wide recognition that many of our children are not learning to act responsibly while they are young. Studies show that many children see nothing wrong with cheating on tests. Some see nothing wrong with taking things that don't belong to them.

If proper attitudes and behavior are not learned early, problems can mushroom with even worse consequences when children are older. As crime has increased, teen-age offenders have shown less and less feeling for their victims. But even for the youngsters who will never commit a crime, it is better to learn responsibility when they are young, rather than when they are older and they have to change bad habits.

This section of the book focuses on practical suggestions for helping young children appreciate the importance of acting responsibly in their everyday lives. Further, it provides ideas on how to help them make responsible choices and stick with them, even when doing so is hard and the material rewards are few.

Many parents will also want to share with their children deeply held religious and moral convictions as a foundation for ethical behavior.

This section discusses habits of fairness, respect, courage, honesty, and compassion that responsible people share and that can be used by parents with different beliefs.

As parents, we can give our children the best in us by helping them acquire habits and character traits that they can rely on in their own lives. If we help them learn to take pleasure in thinking and behaving well, they will have the best chance to lead good lives as individuals and as citizens in the community. This will be true no matter what unpleasant situations or bad influences they come across.

What Do We Mean By Responsible Behavior?

None of us is born acting responsibly. A responsible character is formed over time. It is made up of our outlook and daily habits associated with feelings, thoughts, and actions. Responsible people act the way they should whether or not anyone is watching. They do so because they understand that it's right and because they have the courage and self-control to act decently, even when tempted to do otherwise.

We want our children to appreciate the importance of being responsible. We also want them to develop the habits and strength to act this way in their everyday lives. Learning to be responsible includes learning to:

1. Respect and show compassion for others.
2. Practice honesty as a matter of course.
3. Show courage in standing up for our principles.
4. Develop self-control in acting on our principles.
5. Maintain self-respect.

Respect And Compassion For Others:

As part of being responsible, children need to respect and show concern for the well-being of other people. Respect ranges from using basic manners to having compassion for the suffering of others. Compassion is developed by trying to see things from the point of view of others, and learning that their feelings resemble our own.

"Daddy, why was Granma crying"?

"She is very sad. One of her closest friends just died. Come in and sit with me. Do you remember how you felt when your gerbil,

Whiskers died?"

"I felt sad and lonely."

"I'm sure Granma feels that way, too. Maybe you can think of a way to help her."

"I could give her a hug..."

"That's a great idea! I'm really glad you thought of it."

Respect for others also includes the habit of treating people fairly as individuals, regardless of race, sex, or ethnic group. As we mature, respect includes realizing that not all our obligations to others, such as caring for a family member who is sick, are chosen freely. And it includes tolerance for people who do not share our beliefs or likes or dislikes, as long as they do not harm others.

These habits are especially important because many of the wrongs people commit result from indifference to the suffering they cause.

Honesty:

Honesty means telling the truth. It means not misleading others for our own benefit. It also means trying to make decisions, especially important ones, on the basis of evidence rather than prejudice. Honesty includes dealing with other people and being honest with ourselves.

To understand the importance of being truthful to others, our children need to learn that living together depends on trust. Without honesty, trusting each other becomes impossible. Honesty with ourselves involves facing up to our own mistakes and biases, even when we have to admit them to others. It includes self-criticism. The point is to learn from our errors and to do our best to correct them, not to dwell on them.

Courage:

Courage is taking a position and doing what is right, even at the risk of some loss. It means being neither reckless nor cowardly, but facing up to our duties. It includes physical courage, intellectual courage to make decisions on the basis of evidence, and moral courage to stand up for our principles.

Courage does not mean never being afraid. It can involve trying to overcome our fears, such as a fear of the dark. But our children also need to learn that sometimes it is all right to be afraid.

"Daddy, a man showed us money by the school playground today."

"What did you do?"

"We ran for the teacher."

"Why did you do that?"

"We were scared. You and mommy and our teacher Mrs. Jones said never take any-thing from grownups we don't know. Run away. Go and tell somebody we know."

"Good for you. It was right to be scared. Lots of people are nice but some are very mean. They can hurt you. The mean ones sometimes try to fool people by pretending to be nice. Now, tell me, what did the man look like?"

Courage becomes especially important by the time children become teenagers. They often have to stand up against peer pressure to do the wrong thing, such as using drugs.

Self-Control:

Self-control is the ability to resist inappropriate behavior in order to act responsibly. It relates to all of the different aspects of responsibility mentioned so far, including re-spect and compassion for others, honesty, and courage. It involves persistence and stick-ing to long-term commitments. It also includes dealing effectively with emotions, such as anger, and developing patience.

Self-Respect:

People with self-respect take satisfaction in appropriate behavior and hard-won ac-complishments. They don't need to put others down or have a lot of money in order to respect themselves. People who respect themselves also view selfishness, loss of self-control, recklessness, cowardice, and dishonesty as wrong and unworthy of them. As they mature, if they have learned the lessons of responsibility, they will develop a good conscience to guide them.

In addition, people who respect themselves respect their own health and safety. Simi-larly, they are unwilling to be manipulated by others. Patience or tolerance does not mean allowing others to mistreat us.

While we help children have high standards for themselves, we also need to let them know that failure is no embarrassment when we have done our best. For example, losing a game when we have done our best, and our opponent has simply played better, is no disgrace.

How Can Parents Encourage Responsible Behavior?
Everyday Experiences:

Especially when they are young, children learn best about responsibility in concrete situations. What they do and what they witness have lasting effects. Most of the activities described in this book are for you and your child.

We are always teaching, our children something by our words and our actions. They learn from seeing. They learn from hearing. They learn from overhearing. They learn from us, from each other, from other adults, and by themselves.

All of us acquire habits by doing things over and over again, whether in learning to play a musical instrument, to pick up after ourselves, to play games and sports, or to share with others. The best way to encourage our children to become responsible is to act as responsibly as we can in their presence. We must genuinely try to be the sort of people we hope they will try to become.

We can show them by our words and by our actions that we respect others. We can show them our compassion and concern when others are suffering. They need to see our own self-control, courage, and honesty. They need to learn that we treat ourselves, as well as others, with respect, and that we always try to do our best. As they grow older, they should have the chance to learn why we live as we do.

"Daddy, why are you leaving that note on the garbage can?"

"There is broken glass inside, Matthew, and I don't want the garbage collectors to get hurt because of me, I am warning them about the glass."

"Are they your friends?"

"No. I don't know them."

"But you don't want them to get hurt..."

As our children watch us daily, as we talk to them, encouraging their questions and trying to answer them thoughtfully, they begin to understand us — and we begin to understand them. Understanding each other well is the best way to teach our children respect for our ideals of good character.

Using Literature And Stories:

Children learn about responsibility through many activities, including reading stories. They learn by identifying with individual characters or because the message from a favorite story strikes a particular chord. Children can be touched deeply by good literature, and they may ask to have things read to them again and again. Children can learn all sorts of lessons from stories. They might learn about courage by reading about David standing up to Goliath. Or they might learn the value of persistence and effort from The Little Engine That Could.

When they are older, reading can help prepare children for the realities and responsibilities of adulthood.

When our children grow up they often remember stories that were told to them by family members when they were young. When we tell stories to our children, we should remember old favorites of ours, like the three little pigs, not leaving out a single time the wolf says, "I'LL HUFF, and I'LL PUFF, and I'LL BLOW YOUR HOUSE IN!"

Developing Judgment And Thoughtfulness:

Judgment on ethical issues is a practical matter. Children develop their capacity for judging what is a responsible act, just as they come to appreciate the meaning of responsibility, through practice. Especially when they are young, children need to see moral question in terms that are meaningful to them.

We can also help our children develop good judgment by talking through complicated situations with them. One way is to help them understand the long-term consequences of different choices. If they tell us about a story they have read, we might ask them to imagine what the result might have been if a favorite character had acted differently.

Sometimes, it can be difficult to know the difference between acting bravely and acting recklessly or how to balance duties when they conflict. As parents, we can help by making it clear, through what we do as well as what we say, that it is important in such situations to think carefully and honestly about what should be done, as well as to keep in mind how others will be affected by what we do.

Your child's ability to reason about different issues, including ethical ones, will improve as your child matures. Just as reasoning can lead to a more thoughtful understanding of responsibility, or what actions to take in complicated situations, it may also become easier to rationalize selfish or reckless behavior. But if you have helped your young child develop strong habits of considering the welfare of others, honesty, courage, and admiration for worthy accomplishments, your child will have a solid foundation on which to build.

A) Activities:

As parents, sometimes we think that we must set aside particular times or create special situations in order to teach our children, But that is far from the truth when it comes to learning about responsibility. While it is important to have some times together when you won't be disturbed, the most ordinary situations in everyday life are filled with opportunities for sound teaching, if parents pay attention to them.

This section contains activities to encourage habits of responsibility in your child. Most of them are not, however, the kind of activities that you can do together for half an hour once a week. Instead they are more like rules of thumb, ideas to build on. They illustrate the concepts introduced in the previous sections. They should stimulate your own thinking and your own ideas.

Just remember one thing: teaching our children about responsibility doesn't mean that we can't laugh or that we have to be grim.

Our children should see that we can be serious about our principles, while still being able to play and have fun.

"Dad, can I show you what we did in ballet class today?"

"Sure."

"It was hard. We had to get way up on our toes and then twirl around like this."

"Great. Let me try it...Oops! Now, what's so funny about that? Well, OK. I guess we aren't all as graceful as you are."

Getting To Know Others:

Children need to be shown and taught respect for others. Other people have feelings and hopes, just as we do. We have much to learn from each other — from people who live far away and from those who lived long ago.

What To Do:

1. Set a good example by acting respectfully toward others. Always make clear that prejudice is wrong and that all of us are equals, no matter our color, gender, or background.

2. Show an interest in learning about and from others — from neighbors and relatives, and from books about our own and other civilizations. Tell your child interesting things you have learned

3. Encourage your child to learn about many different lands and people, to learn more than one language, and to read stories about children from all over the world. Show your child how you try to see things from the point of view of others.

4. Listen attentively when your child wants to tell you about interesting things discovered about history, geography, religion, art, and ways of life.

We can help our children understand that there are often things to learn from those who lived in the past and from those whose lives are different from our own. We can teach our children to behave respectfully toward people and not pre-judge them. Sometimes, however, we must make it clear that some people behave in ways that are harmful, and such behavior should not be tolerated.

Magic Words, Caring Deeds:

The magic words are "please" and "thank you". There are other manners we are constantly teaching our children as well.

What To Do:

1. Show your children the manners you expect at home first. The next time you eat dinner together, have the children pretend they are eating in a restaurant. How should they talk to each other? What should they say when the waiter brings their food? Or

have the children pretend they are riding in a bus. What should they do if the bus stops suddenly and they bump into someone? How should they carry a large package on the bus?

2. The next time your children mention something nice that another person did for them, suggest they write a thank you note. It doesn't have to have a lot of words. It can have pictures as well.

3. You, too, can write short notes to your child to indicate your appreciation for something done right.

Children need to learn that little signs of appreciation can be very important to other people. And manners are a part of respecting and caring for the feelings of others. If we turn the chore of learning manners into a game, children will get the practice they need without embarrassing us or themselves. As you teach the importance of manners, you may need to be honest about what your child can expect from others:

"Mom, why do you make such a fuss when I chew with my mouth open?"

"Because it's ugly for other people to see. Good manners show respect for other people."

"What's respect?"

"It means caring how other people feel."

"If I care about them, will they care about me?"

"Not always, Paul. Some people don't care and never will, no matter how kind we are to them. But in our family, we do care."

Gifts From The Heart:

Your child give a gift of himself at the next holiday or any time he wants to do something nice for someone else.

What To Do:

1. Talk to your child about gift giving. What does it mean to give something to someone else?

2. Instead of buying a gift, have your child make a gift. Does your child have a special talent? Maybe your child would like to sing or write a song for a relative? Is there a

chore your child could do? Maybe wash the dishes for a week. Is there a special toy that could be loaned to a sister or brother for a week?

3. Use materials from around the house so that little, if any, money is spent.

4. If the gift is an activity or chore, have your child make a card with a note on it, telling what the gift will be.

5. Have your child use imagination in making an inviting package. Perhaps your child could paint a small rock and wrap it in a box. Or make an envelope out of the comics from the Sunday newspaper.

Most young children don't have money to buy a gift for a friend or relative. You can teach your child that a gift that shows effort and attention can mean more than a gift from the store.

Honesty, The Best Policy:

Children need to learn that benefiting from manipulating or lying to others is dishonest and unworthy of them.

What To Do:

1. Tell the story about the boy who cried "Wolf" so many times to get attention that when the wolf finally came no one believed him.

2. Ask your child if anyone has ever lied to her. How did that make her feel?

3. Be careful to follow through on things you say to your child. Commitments that may seem minor to you can mean a lot to your child. Make promises and keep them.

Our children need to learn about the importance of trusting each other in our everyday lives. Without honesty, trust becomes impossible.

There's A Monster In My Room!

Sometimes our children have needless fears that we can help them overcome.

What To Do:

1. Listen when your child mentions fear, even if it sounds silly to you.

2. With your child, come up with a plan for facing up to the fear.

3. Go through the plan together. Let your child take the step that confronts the fear, although it may be helpful for you to be there.

Our children can acquire courage if we help them gain practice in standing up to their unnecessary fears. In addition, if we take seriously what are real concerns to them, they will trust us and feel safe telling us their thoughts and feelings.

Bully:

Children should learn not to allow others to mistreat them. At the same time, we want them to learn how to reach understandings peacefully, whenever possible.

What To Do:

1. Listen to your child and find out if others are not treating your child as they should. This will encourage your child to trust you and come to you when there is a problem.

2. Help your child consider various ways of dealing with a particular problem.

3. If the problem is the way another child is behaving, suggest working out the problem by talking with the other child, or a responsible adult.

4. If the problem is another adult, however, or if your child is seriously threatened by other children, you will need to intervene directly. A part of self-respect is not tolerating mistreatment by others. Finding appropriate ways to deal with unpleasant behavior by others is an important, if sometimes difficult, part of growing up.

Helping Out:

Our children need to learn that as they get older and can contribute more, more will be expected of them.

What To Do:

1. As your child matures, consider additional ways your child can contribute to the household.

2. Discuss the new duties with your child. Avoid describing them in ways that seem like a punishment. Instead, you can imply that they require a new level of ability, which your child now possesses.

3. With younger children, it helps sometimes if you do the chores together and talk or make fun. But don't do your child's work!

4. If possible, new task should stretch a child's abilities and encourage satisfaction in good work. Praise something done well, especially a new challenge.

Doing chores is a useful way to learn persistence and to learn that when we live up to our responsibilities we enable others to trust and rely on us.

A Job Well Done:

We need to show our children that we take satisfaction in acting properly and accomplishing difficult tasks.

What To Do:

1. Through your daily activities, show your children that you care about a job well done.

2. Perhaps our children's most important tasks are to work hard at school and do homework. When we check homework and point out mistakes, we help them see how an error has arisen. When we let them correct errors themselves, we inspire self-confidence. It is also important for us to show them that we appreciate their good efforts.

3. Teaching our children self-respect does not mean complimenting everything they do. Our children also need our honest criticism from time to time. When we do criticize, it should be of things they have done, not about them personally.

4. Most of all, we should help our children form the self-confidence and self-respect that come from opportunities to do good work as students or as family members.

Helping our children form self-respect is based on how we treat them and our own example. There are many opportunities to teach self-respect through our actions:

"Dad, nobody's going to see inside the model's wing. Why do you work so hard with all those little pieces?"

"Because that's the way to build the plane, Martha. It makes the wing strong when the plane flies, and that's more important than what people see. I want to make the best plane I can. Do you want to help?"

Our Heroes:

Many children love to look at portraits or photographs, especially if you can tell them stories about the people in the pictures.

What To Do:

1. Select a photo of a person in your family with an impressive quality or accomplishment. Tell your child about the person and about what the person did. Perhaps your grandparents had the courage to emigrate from another country or your parents sacrificed in order to support you in school. Talk about the results of these actions.

2. Collect photographs from newspapers or magazines about impressive people in your community. With your child, talk about their actions that merit admiration or praise.

3. In addition to relatives or others, you may want to display portraits of other people who deserve our admiration and respect. A, picture of Anne Frank, a young girl who wrote a diary while she and her family lived in hiding from Nazi Germans and who died in a concentration camp, can inspire conversation about courage and compassion for others. A portrait of Martin Luther King, a great civil rights leader who believed in nonviolent change, can lead to discussions of great accomplishment despite prejudice. Choose people whom you admire and feel comfortable talking to your child about.

By the stories we tell about the people we admire, we can inspire children and remind them of those qualities we think are important.

OOPS!

Sometimes, as parents, we don't act the way we should in front of our children.

What To Do:

1. Try to be honest with yourself and your child if you find that you've done something that sets a bad example. Sometimes we need to think a little about an event to realize that we've done something inappropriate,

2. If your child has observed your behavior it's especially important that you be honest. A simple statement is appropriate in most cases; there is no need to turn your admission into a major event.

3. Follow up with an apology to anyone you have treated badly and, if possible, by making up for what you have done.

It's important that our children, especially older ones, see that we face up to our own mistakes.

Will You Be My Friend?

Our children need to learn to choose their friends wisely.

What To Do:

1. Talk to your child about what is important in a friend. In addition to being fun, what other qualities are important? What about honesty, dependability, a real interest in your child's welfare?

2. Talk to your child about the type of friends to avoid. Ask if your child can remember a friend who couldn't be counted on.

    Our children should learn that it is important to choose friends and companions who care about others and act responsibly.

Share A Story:

One important way parents can help their children learn respect for others, self-control, or other aspects of responsibility is through the use of fables or stories. You can read to your child, you can read with your child and you can encourage your child to read on his own.

What To Do:

1. Turn off the TV or other distractions.

2. Find stories that exemplify important aspects of character and that your child might enjoy.

3. Talk to your child about the behavior of different character in the story. Ask your child how some of the behavior might apply to your own lives.

4. Share some stories or books that you have found meaningful with your child. (It is important for your child to see you reading and enjoying stories as well.)

5. Come up with your own stories. These can be family stories, such as baby stories (when your child was little...) that can become a part of your child's personal history.

    Stories can be good ways to learn important lessons. Your child can identify with characters in meaningful situations without your having to lecture.

B) Parents And The Schools:

Parents need to work with teachers and other parents to ensure that children are brought up well. An African proverb says, "It takes an entire village to raise one child." It is important for parents and other adults to cooperate in order to have common goals for them. Close communication is essential.

Parents can visit with teachers to discuss ways they and the school can reinforce the same lesson about good character. Children are less likely to do much homework, for example, if parents let them watch television for hours.

Parents can learn from teachers what their children are studying and what interests them. A teacher or school librarian can provide good ideas for activities to do at home.

Parents can cooperate with each other, too. They can agree on standards of supervision at parties and on entertainment. Some parents may be free to escort children to museums, libraries, athletic events, and extracurricular school activities, when others are not. Taking turns can provide better opportunities for all the children.

Part 6
Children And Drugs
A Plan For Achieving Schools Without Drugs:
What Can We Do?

Parents:

1. Teach standards of right and wrong, and demonstrate these standards through personal example.

2. Help children to resist peer pressure to use alcohol and other drugs by supervising their activities, knowing who their friends are, and talking with them about their interests and problems,

3. Be knowledgeable about drugs and signs of drug use. When symptoms are observed, respond promptly.

Schools:

4. Determine the extent and character of alcohol and other drug use and monitor that use regularly.

5. Establish clear and specific rules regarding alcohol and other drug use that include strong corrective actions.

6. Enforce established policies against drug use fairly and consistently. Ensure adequate security measures to eliminate drugs from school premises and school functions.

7. Implement a comprehensive drug prevention curriculum for kindergarten through grade 12, teaching that drug use is wrong and harmful, and supporting and strengthening resistance to drugs.

8. Reach out to the community for support and assistance in making the school's anti-drug policy and program work. Develop collaborative arrangements in school personnel, parents, school boards, law enforcement officers, treatment organizations, and private groups to work together to provide necessary resources.

Students:

9. Learn about the effects of alcohol and other drug use, the reasons why drugs are harmful, and. ways to resist pressures to try drugs.

10. Use an understanding of the danger posed by alcohol and other drugs to help other students avoid them. Encourage other students to resist drugs, persuade those using

drugs to seek help, and report those selling drugs to parents and the school principal.

Communities:

11. Help schools fight drugs by providing them with the expertise and financial resources of community groups and agencies.

12. Involve local law enforcement agencies in all aspects of drug prevention: assessment, enforcement, and education. The police and courts should have well-established relationships with the schools.

"I felt depressed and hurt all the time. I hated myself for the way I hurt my parents and treated them so cruelly, and for the way I treated others. I hated myself the most, though, for the way I treated myself. I would take drugs until I overdosed, and fell further and further behind in school and work and relationships with others. I just didn't care anymore whether I lived or died. I stopped going to school altogether... I felt constantly depressed and began having thoughts of suicide which scared me a lot! I didn't know where to turn..."

— Stewart, a high school student

Children And Drugs:

When 13- to 18-year-olds were asked to name the biggest problem facing young people today, drug use led the list. In 1987 54 percent of teens cited drugs as their greatest concern — up from 27 percent only 10 years earlier.

Eighty-nine percent of teens oppose legalization of marijuana, and 77 percent believe it would be wrong to decriminalize the possession of small amounts of marijuana.

Drugs and alcohol rank high on the list of topics that teens wish they could discuss more with their parents — 42 percent want more   discussions with parent about drugs, and 39 percent feel the need to talk about drinking.

— The Gallup Youth Surveys, 1987 and 1988

Schools and Drugs:

Americans have consistently identified drug use among the top problems confronting the nation's schools. Yet many do not recognize the, degree to which their own children, their own schools, and their own communities are at risk.

Research shows that drug use among children is 10 times more prevalent than parents suspect. In addition, many students know that their parents do not recognize the extent of drug use; as a result, some young people believe that they can use drug with impunity.

School administrators and teachers often are unaware that some of their students are using and selling drugs on school property. As Ralph Egers, former superintendent of schools in South Portland, Maine, put it, "We'd like to think that our kids don't have this problem, but the brightest kid from the best family in the community could have the problem."

The Facts Are:

1. Drug use is not confined to young people in certain geographic areas or from particular economic backgrounds; drug use affects young people throughout the nation.

2. Drugs are a serious problem not only among high school students but among middle and elementary school students as well.

3. Heavy drinking, defined as five or more drinks on one occasion, is reported by 30 percent of high school seniors, and more than one-half occasional users of alcohol.

4. All illegal drugs are dangerous; there is no such thing as safe or responsible use of illegal drugs.

5. Although drug trafficking is controlled by adults, the immediate source of drugs for most students is other students.

Continuing misconceptions about the drug problem stand in the way of corrective action. The following section outlines the nature and extent of the problem and summarizes the latest research on the effects of drugs on students and schools.

Extent Of Alcohol And Other Drug Use:

The drug problem affects all types of students. All regions and all types of communities show high levels of drug use. Thirty percent of 1990 high school seniors in nonmetropolitan areas reported illicit drug use in the previous year, while the rate for seniors in large metropolitan areas was 33 percent. Although higher porportions of males are involved in illicit drug use, especially heavy drug use, the gap between the sexes is closing. The extent to which high school seniors, reported having used illicit drugs is higher for whites than for blacks.

Drug use is widespread among American schoolchildren. Although a national study of high school seniors in 1991 shows that drug use among young people is declining, the figures remain unacceptably high. The United States continues to have the highest rate of teenage drug use of any nation in the industrialized world. Forty-four percent of high school seniors have tried an illicit drug by the time they graduate Alcohol is the most widely used drug. By their senior year, 88 percent of students in the class of 1991 had used alcohol; 78 percent had used alcohol in the past year and 54 percent had used it in the month prior to the survey. Thirty percent of seniors surveyed reported at least one occasion of heavy drinking in the two weeks prior to the survey — an occasion in which they had five or more drinks in a row. Twenty-four percent of 1991 seniors reported using marijuana in the past year, and 14 percent said they had used it at least once in the previous month. Three and one-half percent of seniors indicated that they had used cocaine in the past year. Three percent of seniors had used crack, and 1.5 percent had used it within the last year.

Initial use of alcohol and other drugs occurs at an increasingly early age. Nineteen percent of seniors report they had initiated cigarette use by the sixth grade and 11 percent had used alcohol. Forty-four percent of 8th graders have tried cigarettes and 70 percent have at least tried alcohol. Twenty-seven percent of 8th graders have gotten drunk at least once, and 13 percent report they have consumed five or more drinks in a row. Of the illicit drugs, marijuana and inhalants show the earliest pattern of initiation; about 2.8 percent of seniors had begun using both of these substances by the sixth grade. The peak initiation rate is reached by the 9th grade. Peak initiation rates for cocaine and hallucinogens are reached in 10th and 11th grade with the initiation rate for nearly all drugs falling off by the 12th grade.

Fact Sheet; Drugs And Dependence:

Drugs cause physical and emotional dependence. Users may develop a craving for specific drugs, and their bodies may respond to the presence of drugs in ways that lead to increased drug use.

Regular users of drugs develop tolerance, a need to take larger doses to get the same initial effect. They may respond by combining drugs, frequently with devastating results. Many teenage drug users calling a national cocaine hotline report that they take other drugs just to counteract the unpleasant effects of cocaine.

Certain drugs such as opiates, barbituates, alcohol and nicotine, create physical dependence. With prolonged use, these drugs become part of the body chemistry. When a regular user stops taking the drug, the body experiences the physiological trauma known as withdrawal.

Psychological dependence occurs when taking drugs becomes the center of the user's life. Among children, psychological dependence erodes school performance and can destroy ties to family and friends, as well as cause the child to abandon outside interests, values, and goals. The child goes from taking drugs to feel good, to taking them to keep from feeling bad. Over time, drug use itself heightens the bad feelings can leave the user suicidal. More than half of all adolescent suicides are drug related.

Drugs can remain in the body long after use has stopped. The extent to which a drug is retained in the body depends on the drug's chemical composition, that is, whether it is fat-soluble. Fat-soluble drugs such as marijuana and phencyclidine (PCP) seek out and settle in the fatty tissues. As a result, they build up in the fatty parts of the body such as the brain. Such accumulations of drugs and their slow release over time may have effects on the mind and body weeks or even months after drug use has stopped.

How Drug Use Develops:

Social influence play a key role in making drug use attractive to children. The first temptations to use drugs may come in social situations in the form of pressures to "act grown up" by smoking cigarettes or using alcohol or marijuana.

A 1987 Weekly Reader survey found that television and movies had the greatest influence on fourth through sixth graders in making drugs and alcohol seem attractive; the second greatest influence was other children.

The survey offers insights into why students take drugs. Children in grades four through six think that the most important reason for using alcohol and, marijuana is to "fit in with others," followed closely by a desire "to feel older." Students also have in-complete or inaccurate information. For example, only 44 percent of six graders polled in a national survey think alcohol should be called a drug. This finding reinforces the need for prevention programs beginning in the early grades — programs that focus on teach-ing children the facts about drugs and alcohol and the skills to resist peer pressure to use them.

Students who turn to more potent drugs usually do so after first using cigarettes and alcohol and then marijuana. Initial attempts may not produce a "high"; however, students who continue to use drugs learn that drugs can change their thoughts and feelings. The greater a student's involvement with marijuana, the more likely it is the student , will begin to use other drugs in conjunction with marijuana.

Drug use frequently progresses in stages — from occasional use, to regular, use to multiple drug use, and ultimately to total dependency. With each successive stage, drug use intensifies, becomes more varied, and results in increasingly debilitating effects,

But this progression is not inevitable. Drug use can be stopped at any stage. However, the more deeply involved children are with drugs, the more difficult it is for them to stop. The best way to fight drug use is to begin prevention efforts before children start using drugs. Prevention efforts that focus on young children are the most effective means to fight drug use.

Fact Sheet; Youth And Alcohol:

Alcohol is the number one drug problem among youth. The easy availability, widespread acceptability, and extensive promotion of alcoholic beverages within our society make alcohol the most widely used and abused drug.

Alcohol use is widespread. By their senior year of high school nearly 90 percent of students will have tried alcoholic beverages. Despite a legal drinking age of 21, junior and senior high school students drink 35 percent Of all wine coolers sold in the United States. They also drink an estimated 1.1 billion bottles and cans of beer each year.

Drinking has acute effects on the body. The heavy, fast-paced drinking that young people commonly engage in quickly alters judgment, vision, coordination, and speech and often leads to dangerous risk-taking behavior. Because young people have lower body weight than adults, youth absorb alcohol into their blood system faster than adults and exhibit greater impairment for longer periods of time. Alcohol use not only increases the likelihood of being involved in an accident, it increases the risk of serious injury in an accident because of its harmful effects on numerous parts of the body.

Alcohol-related highway accidents are the principal cause of death among young people ages 15 through 24. Alcohol use is the primary cause of traffic accidents involving teenage drivers. Furthermore, about half of all youthful deaths in drowning, fires, suicide, and homicide are alcohol-related.

Any alcoholic beverage can be misused. Contrary to popular belief, drinking beer or wine can have effects similar to drinking "hard" liquor. A bottle of beer, a glass of wine, or a bottle of wine cooler have about the same amount of ethyl alcohol as a drink made with liquor. Those who drive "under the influence" are most likely to have been drinking beer.

Early alcohol use is associated with subsequent alcohol dependence and related health problems. Youth who use alcohol at a younger age are more likely to use alcohol heavily and to experience alcohol-related problems affecting their relationships with family and friends by late adolescence. Their school performance is likely to suffer, and they are more likely to be truant. They are also more likely to abuse other drugs and to get in trouble with the law, or, if they are girls, to become pregnant.

Effects Of Drug Use:

The drugs students are taking today are more potent, more dangerous, and more addictive than ever. Adolescents are particularly vulnerable to the effects of drugs. Drugs threaten normal development in a number of ways:

1. Drugs can interfere with memory, sensation, and perception. They distort experiences and cause a loss of self-control that can lead users to harm themselves and others.

2. Drugs interfere with the brain's ability to take in, sort and synthesize information. As a result, sensory information runs together, providing new sensations while blocking normal ability to understand the information received.

3. Drugs can have an insidious effect on perception; for example, cocaine and amphetamines often give users a false sense of functioning at their best while on the drug.

Drug suppliers have responded to the increasing demand for drugs by developing new strains, producing reprocessed, purified drugs, and using underground laboratories to create more powerful forms of illegal drugs. Consequently, users are exposed to heightened or unknown levels of risk.

The marijuana produced today is from 5 to 20 times stronger than that available as recently as 10 years ago. Regular use by adolescents has been associated with an "amotivational syndrome," characterized by apathy and loss of goals. Research has shown that severe psychological damage, including paranoia and psychosis, can occur when marijuana contains 2 percent THC, its major psychoactive ingredient. Since the early 1980s, most marijuana has contained from 4 to 6 percent THC — two or three times the amount capable of causing serious damage.

Crack is purified and highly addictive form of cocaine. Phencyclidine (PCP), first developed as an animal tranquilizer, has unpredictable and often violent effects. Often children do not even know that they are using this drug when PCP-laced parsley in cigarette form is passed off as marijuana, or when PCP in crystal form is sold as lysergic acid (LSD).

Some of the "designer" drugs, slight chemical variations of existing illegal drugs, have been known to cause permanent brain damage with a single dose.

Fact Sheet; Cocaine - Crack

Cocaine is readily available. Fifty-one percent of seniors say it would be easy for them to get cocaine. Most alarming is the ready availability of cocaine in a cheap but potent form called crack or rock. Crack is a purified form of cocaine that is smoked.

Crack is inexpensive to try. Crack is available for as little as $5. As a result, the drug is affordable to many potential users, including high school and elementary school students.

Crack is easy to use. It is sold in pieces resembling small white gravel or soap chips and is sometimes pressed into small pellets. Crack can be smoked in a, pipe or put into a cigarette. The visible effects disappear within minutes after smoking, so detection is difficult.

Crack is extremely addictive. Crack is far more addictive than heroin or barbiturates. Because crack is smoked, it is quickly absorbed into the blood stream. It produces a feeling of extreme euphoria, peaking within seconds. Repeated use of crack can lead to addiction within a few days.

Crack leads to crime and severe psychological disorders. Many youths, once addicted, have turned to stealing, prostitution, and drug dealing in order to support their habit. Continued use can produce violent behavior and psychotic states similar to schizophrenia.

Crack is deadly. Cocaine in any form, including crack, can cause sudden death from cardiac arrest or respiratory failure.

Drug Use And Learning:

Drugs erode the self-discipline and motivation necessary for learning. Pervasive drug use among students creates a climate in the schools that is destructive to learning.

Research shows that drug use can cause a decline in academic performance. This has been found to be true for students who excelled in school prior to drug use as well as for those with academic or behavioral problems prior to use. According to one study, students using marijuana were twice as likely to average D's and F's as other students. The decline in grades often reverses when drug use is stopped.

Drug use is closely tied to being truant and dropping out of school. High school seniors who are heavy drug users are more than three times as likely to skip school as nonusers. About one-fifth of heavy users skipped three or more school days a month, more than six times the truancy rate of nonusers. In a Philadelphia study, dropouts were almost twice as likely to be frequent drug users as were high school graduates; four in five dropouts used drugs regularly.

Drug use is associated with crime and misconduct that disrupt the maintenance of an orderly and safe school atmosphere conducive to learning. Drugs not only transform schools into marketplaces for dope deals, they also lead to the destruction of property and to classroom disorder. Among high school seniors, heavy drug users were more than three times as likely to vandalize school property and twice as likely to have been involved in a fight at school or at work as nonusers. Students on drugs create a climate of apathy disruption, and disrespect for others. For example, among teenage callers to a national cocaine hotline, 32 percent reported that they sold drugs, and 64 percent said that they stole from family, friends, or employers to buy drugs. A drug-ridden environment is a strong deterrent to learning not only for drug users but for other students as well.

A)   A Plan For Action:

To combat student drug use most effectively, the entire community must be involved: parents, schools, students, law enforcement authorities, religious groups, social service agencies, and the media. They all must transmit a single consistent message that drug use is wrong and dangerous, and it will not be tolerated. This message must be reinforced through strong, consistent law enforcement and disciplinary measures.

The following recommendations and examples describe actions that can be taken by parents, schools, students, and communities to stop drug use. These recommendations are derived from research and from the experiences of schools throughout the country. They show that the drug problem can be overcome.

B) What Parents Can Do:

1. Teach standards of right and wrong, and demonstrate these standards through personal example. Arrange for your child to attend church regularly. It is very important that your child know GOD. A religious background is very important, it will teach your child to respect himself and others as well.

2. Help children to resist peer pressure to use alcohol and other drugs by supervising their activities, knowing who their friends are and talking with them about their interests and problems.

3. Be knowledgeable about drugs and signs of drug use. When symptoms are observed, respond promptly.

Instilling Responsibility:

Teach standards of right and wrong and demonstrate these standards through personal example.

Children who are brought up to value individual responsibility and self-discipline and to have a clear sense of right and wrong are less likely to try drugs than those who are not. Parents can help instill these values by:

1. Arranging for their child to attend church regularly.
2. Setting a good example for children and not using drugs themselves.
3. Explaining to their children at an early age that drug use is wrong, harmful and unlawful, and reinforcing this teaching throughout adolescence.
4. Encouraging self-discipline by giving children regular duties and holding them accountable for their actions.
5. Establishing standards of behavior concerning drugs, drinking, dating, curfews, and unsupervised activities, and enforcing them consistently and fairly.
6. Encouraging their children to stand by their convictions when pressured to use drugs.

Supervising Activities:

Help children to resist peer pressure to use alcohol and other drugs by supervising their activities, knowing who their friends are, and talking with them about their interests and problems.

When parents take an active interest in their children's behavior, they provide the guidance and support children need to resist drugs. Parents can do this by:

1. Knowing their children's whereabouts, activities, and friends.
2. Working to maintain and improve family communications and listening to their children.
3. Communicating regularly With the parents of their children's friends and sharing their knowledge about drugs with other parents.
4. Being able to discuss drugs knowledgeably. It is far better for children to obtain their information from their parents than from their peers or on the streets.
5. Being selective about their children's viewing of television and movies that portray drug use as glamorous or exciting.

In Addition, Parents Can Work With The School To Fight Drugs By:

1. Encouraging the development of a school policy with a clear no-use message.
2. Supporting administrators who are tough on drugs.
3. Assisting the school in monitoring students' attendance and planning and chaperoning school-sponsored activities.
4. Communicating regularly with the school regarding their children's behavior.

Fact Sheet; Signs Of Drug Use:

Changing patterns of performance, appearance, and behavior may signal use of drugs. The items in the first category listed below provide direct evidence of drug use; the items in the other categories offer signs that may indicate drug use. Adults should watch for extreme changes in children's behavior, changes that together form a pattern associated with drug use.

Signs Of Drugs And Drug Paraphernalia:

1. Possession of drug-related paraphernalia such as pipes, rolling papers, small decongestant bottles, eye drops, or small butane torches.
2. Possession of drugs or evidence of drugs, such as pills, white powder, small glass vials, or hypodermic needles; peculiar plants or butts, seeds, or leaves in ashtrays or in clothing pockets.

3.   Odor of drugs, smell of incense or other "cover-up" scents.

Identification With Drug Culture:

1.   Drug-related magazines, slogans on clothing.

2.   Conversation and jokes that are preoccupied with drugs.

3.   Hostility in discussing drugs.

4.   Collection of beer cans.

Signs Of Physical Deterioration:

1.   Memory lapses, short attention span, difficulty in concentration.

2.   Poor physical coordination, slurred or incoherent speech.

3.   Unhealthy appearance, indifference to hygiene and grooming.

4.   Bloodshot eyes, dilated pupils.

Dramatic Changes In School Performance:

1.   Marked downturn in student's grades — not just from C's to F's, but from A's to B's and C's; assignments not completed.

2.   Increased absenteeism or tardiness.

Change In Behavior:

1.   Chronic dishonesty (lying, stealing, cheating,); trouble with the police.

2.   Changes in friends, evasiveness in talking, about new ones.

3.   Possession of large amounts of money.

4.   Increasing and inappropriate anger, hostility, irritability, secretiveness.

5.   Reduced motivation, energy, self-discipline, self-esteem.

6.   Diminished interest in extracurricular activities and hobbies.

Recognizing Drug Use:

Be knowledgeable about drugs and signs of drug use. When symptoms are observed, respond promptly.

Parents are in the best position to recognize early signs of drug use in their children. To inform and involve themselves, parents should take the following steps:

1.   Learn about the extent of the drug problem in their community and in their children's schools.

2.   Learn how to recognize signs of drug use.

3.   Meet with parents of their children's friends or classmates about the drug problem

at their school. Establish a means of sharing information to determine which children are using drugs and who is supplying them.

Parents who suspect their children are using drugs often must deal with their own emotions of anger, resentment, and guilt. Frequently they deny the evidence and postpone confronting their children. Yet, the earlier a drug problem is detected and faced the less difficult it is to overcome. If parents suspect their children are using drugs, they should take the following steps:

1. Devise a plan of action. Consult with school officials and other parents.
2. Discuss their suspicions with their children in a calm, objective manner. Do not confront a child while he or she is under the influence of alcohol or other drugs.
3. Impose disciplinary measures that help remove the child from those circumstances where drug use might occur.
4. Seek advice and assistance from drug treatment professionals and from a group.

C) **What Schools Can Do:**

1. Determine the extent and character of alcohol and other drug use and monitor that use regularly.
2. Establish clear and specific rules regarding alcohol and other drug use that includes strong corrective actions.
3. Enforce established policies against alcohol and other drug use fairly and consistently. Ensure adequate security measures to eliminate drugs from school premises and school functions.
4. Implement a comprehensive drug prevention curriculum for kindergarten through grade 12, teaching that drug use is wrong and harmful, and supporting and strengthening resistance to drugs.
5. Reach out to the community for support and assistance in making the school's anti-drug policy and program work. Develop collaborative arrangements in which school personnel, parents, school boards, law enforcement officers, treatment organizations, and private groups can work together to provide necessary resources.

Assessing The Problem:

Determine the extent and character of alcohol and other drug use and monitor that use regularly.

School personnel should be informed about the extent of drugs in their school. School boards, superintendents, and local public officials should support school administrators in their effort to assess the extent of the drug problem and to combat it.

To guide and evaluate effective drug prevention efforts, schools need to take, the following actions:

1. Conduct anonymous surveys of students and school personnel and consult with local law enforcement officials to identify the extent of the drug problem.

2. Bring together school personnel to identify areas where drugs are being used and sold.

3. Meet with parents to help determine the nature and extent of drug use.

4. Maintain records on drug use and sale in the school over time, for use in evaluating and improving drug prevention efforts. In addition to self-reported drug use patterns, records may include information on drug-related arrests and school discipline problems.

5. Inform the community, in straightforward language, of the results of the school's assessment of the drug problem.

Roncalli, High School
Manitowoc, Wisconsin:

Before Roncalli, a Catholic coed high school, initiated its no-use drug policy in the early 1980s, it was not uncommon after athletic events to see a parking lot full of empty beer cans and to hear reports of students charged with driving while intoxicated.

After an alcohol-related teenage traffic fatality jolted the community, a district-wide survey was taken that showed widespread drug and alcohol used by high school students. The Roncalli student body was no exception. In response, an action plan was developed by students, parents, and the community that calls for referral and treatment on the first offense for any student found in the possession of or under the influence of alcohol or drugs at any Roncalli High School activity. The consequence for a second offense is dismissal.

Since this program's inception 13 years ago, only one student has declined referral and treatment, choosing instead to leave school. Tracking surveys each year help the faculty and students to monitor progress in achieving the school's drug free goal.

Positive peer pressure and team spirit are important ingredients in Roncalli's anti-

drug program. The student group RADD (Roncalli Against Drinking and Drugs) oper-
ates as an arm of the Student Senate to organize and coordinate drug-free activities through
the year. More than 90 percent of the 650 students at Roncalli High participate in RADD's
activities that include dances, open gym, Trivial Pursuit contest, Pictionary night, video
screenings, and other after-school events.

A Peer Helpers program matches all 120 incoming freshmen with peers who provide
information throughout the year on Roncalli's anti-drug policies and program.

Concerned Persons Groups also meet at Roncalli to offer extra peer support to students who have a friend or family member using drugs or who may need a place to talk
and find assistance in confidence. The groups meet during the school day on alternating
schedules so that all may have the option to attend.

Parents, too, are actively involved, in the school program. The Roncallli Parents,
too, are actively involved in, the school program.The Roncalli Parents Communication
Network has commitments from more than 60 percent of the Roncalli parents to keep
their homes drug free and to be present when students visit.

Setting Policy:

Establish clear and specific rules regarding alcohol and other drug use that include
strong corrective actions.

School policies should clearly establish that drug use, possession, and sale on the
school grounds and at school functions will not be tolerated. These policies should apply
both to students and to school personnel, and may include prevention, intervention, treatment, and disciplinary measures.

School policies should have the following characteristics:

1. Specify what constitutes a drug offense by defining:

    A) Illegal substances and paraphernalia.

    B) The area of the school's jurisdiction, for example, the school property, its sur-
        roundings, and all school-related events, such as proms and football games.

    C) The types of violations (drug possession, use, and sale).

2. State the consequences for violating school policy; punitive action should be linked
    to referral for treatment and counseling.

    Measures that schools have found effective in dealing with first time offenders include the following:

A) A required meeting of parents and the student with school officials, concluding with a contract signed by the student and parents in which they both acknowledge a drug problem and the student agrees to stop using and to participate in drug counseling or a rehabilitation program.

B) Suspension, assignment to an alternative school, in-school suspension. after-school or Saturday detention with close supervision, and demanding academic assignments.

C) Referral to a drug treatment expert or counselor.

D) Notification of police.

Penalties for repeeat offenders and for sellers may include expulsion, legal action and referral for treatment.

3. Describe procedures for handing violations, including the following:

A) Legal issues associated with disciplinary action, (confidentiality, due process, and search and seizure) and their application.

B) Circumstances under which incidents should be reported and the responsibilities and procedures for reporting incidents, including the identification of the authorities to be contacted.

C) Procedures for notifying parents when their child is suspected of using drugs or caught with drugs.

D) Procedures for notifying police.

4. Enlist legal counsel to ensure that all policy is in compliance with applicable federal, state, and local laws.

5. Building community support for the policy. Hold open meetings where views can be aired and differences resolved.

Enforcing School Policy:

Enforce established policies against alcohol and other drug use fairly and consistently. Ensure adequate security measures to eliminate drugs from school premises and school functions.

Ensure that everyone understands the policy and the procedures that will be followed in case of infractions. Make copies of the school policy available to all parents, teachers, and students, and publicize the policy throughout the school and community.

Impose strict security measures to bar access to intruders and to prohibit student drug trafficking. Enforcement policies should correspond to the severity of the school's drug problem. For example:

1. Officials can require students to carry hall passes, supervise school grounds and hallways, and secure assistance of law enforcement officials particularly to help monitor areas around the school.

2. For a severe drug problem, officials can use security personnel to monitor closely all school areas where sales and use are known to occur; issue mandatory identification badges for school staff and students; request the assistance of local police to help stop drug dealing; and depending on applicable law, develop a policy that permit periodic searches of student lockers.

Review enforcement practices regularly to ensure that penalties are uniformly and fairly applied.

3. Consider implementing an alternative program for students who have been suspended for drug use or possession. Some districts have developed off-campus programs to enable suspended students to continue their education in a more tightly structured environment. These programs may be offered during the day or in the evening, and may offer counseling as well as an academic curriculum. Other districts have successfully used a probationary alternative that combined a short-term in-school suspension with requirements for drug testing and participation in support groups as a condition of returning to the classroom.

Lawrence Middle School
Lawrenceville, Georgia

Ten years ago, Lawrenceville, Georgia, was a rural community outside Atlanta. Today it is a full-fledged suburb, and one of the nation's fastest-growing. Lawrenceville Middle School, responding to rapid changes in the community, did not wait for a crisis to begin thinking about the drug education needs of its 1,100 students. It conducted a survey in 1981 to use as a benchmark to measure drug-free progress in subsequent years and to help define an appropriate program — the first in Gwinnett County — for sixth-, seventh-, and eight-graders.

The Lawrenceville program emphasizes five prevention strategies: education, life and social skills, healthy alternatives, risk factor

Reduction, and environmental change. While annual surveys help the faculty and parents assess its effectiveness, they are not the only way they measure effectiveness. Regular informal assessments and day-to-day faculty observation help to fine tune the program from year to year and suggest any immediate changes required. A case in point: when teachers begin to observe an increase in tobacco use, particularly smokeless tobacco use. They formed a committee that included parents and administrators and came up with a plan to include more information in the curriculum on the harmful effects of tobacco and more up-to-date materials in the media center. They also decided to implement a no-tobacco use policy for the school staff. The following year, incidents of student tobacco use decreased dramatically.

Parents, students, and teachers attribute much of Lawrenceville's drug education success to its alternative program, STRIDE, (Student/ Teacher Resource Institute for Drug Education), a unique concept that has captured the attention — and drug-free pledges — of more than 80 percent of Lawrenceville's students.

STRIDE's leadership team — composed of seventh- and eighth-graders — meets during the summer to plan activities for the upcoming year. A program featuring 10 to 12 major events is outlined at the summer planning session. STRIDE leaders meet regularly during the school year to implement the program and delegate responsibilities. STRIDE events — held after school from 2:00 to 5:00 — are widely publicized by STRIDE members. Events include programs by visiting athletes who qualify as role models, dances, videos, plays, speakers from the community, and special sports events.

Teaching about Drug Prevention:

Implement a comprehensive drug prevention curriculum for kindergarten through grade 12, teaching that drug use is wrong and harmful, and supporting and strengthening resistance to drugs.

A model program would have these objectives:

1. To value and maintain sound personal health.
2. To respect laws and rules prohibiting drugs.
3. To resist pressures to use drugs.
4. To promote student activities that are drug free and offer healthy avenues for stu-

dent interests.

In developing a program, school staff should take the following steps:

1. Determine curriculum content appropriate for the school's drug program and grade levels.

2. Base the curriculum on an understanding of why children try drugs in order to teach them how to resist pressures to use drugs.

3. Review existing materials for possible adaptation. State and national organizations — and some lending libraries — which have an interest in drug prevention make available lists of materials.

In implementing a program, school staff should take the following steps:

1. Include students in all grades. Effective drug education is cumulative.

2. Teach about drugs in health education classes, and reinforce this curriculum with appropriate materials in classes such as social studies and science.

3. Develop expertise in drug prevention through training. Teachers should be knowledgeable about drugs, personally committed to opposing drug use, and skilled at eliciting participation by students in drug prevention efforts.

Fact Sheet; Tips For Selecting Drug Prevention Materials:

In evaluating drug prevention materials, keep the following points in mind: check the publication date. Material published before 1980 may be outdated; even recently published materials may be inaccurate.

Look for "warning flag" phases and concepts. The following expressions, many of which appear frequently in "pro-drug" material, falsely imply that there is a "safe" use of mind-altering drugs: experimental use, recreational use, social use, controlled use, responsible use, use/abuse.

Mood-altering is a deceptive euphemism for mind-altering. The implication of the phase mood-altering is that only temporary feelings are involved. The fact is that mood changes are biological changes in the brain.

"There are no 'good' or 'bad' drugs, just improper use." This is a popular semantic camouflage in pro-drug literature. It confuses young people and minimizes the distinct chemical differences among substances.

"The child's own decision." Parents cannot afford to leave such hazardous choices to their children. It is the parents' responsibility to do all in their power to provide the information and the protection to assure their children a drug-free childhood and adolescence.

Be alert for contradictory messages. Many authors give a pro-drug message and then cover their tracks by including "cautions" about how to use drugs.

Make certain that the health consequences revealed in current research are adequately described. Literature should make these facts clear; the high potency of marijuana on the market today makes it more dangerous than ever. THC, a psychoactive ingredient in marijuana, is fat-soluble, and its accumulation in the body has many adverse biological effects. Cocaine can cause death and is one of the most addictive drugs known. It takes less alcohol to produce impairment in youths than in adults.

Demand material that sets positive standards of behavior for children. The message conveyed must be an expectation that children can say no to drugs. The publication and its message must provide the information and must support family involvement to reinforce the child's courage to stay drug free.

Enlisting The Community's Help:

Reach out to the community for support and assistance in making the school's anti-drug policy and program work. Develop collaborative arrangements in which school personnel, parents, school boards, law enforcement officers, treatment organizations, and private groups can work together to provide resources.

School officials should recognize that they cannot solve the drug problem by themselves. They need to enlist the community's support for their efforts by taking the following actions:

1. Increase community understanding of the problem through meetings, media coverage, and education programs.
2. Build public support for the policy; develop agreement on the goals of a school drug policy, including prevention and enforcement goals.
3. Educate the community about the effects and extent of the drug problem.
4. Strengthen contacts with law enforcement agencies through discussions about the school's specific drug problems and ways they can assist in drug education and enforcement.

5. Call on local professionals, such as physicians and pharmacists, to share their expertise on drug abuse as class lecturers.

6. Mobilize the resources of community groups and local businesses to support the program.

Fact Sheet; Legal Questions On Search And Seizure:

In 1985, the Supreme Court for the first time analyzed the application in public school setting of the Fourth Amendment prohibition of unreasonable searches and seizures. The Court sought to craft a rule that would balance the need of school authorities to maintain order and the privacy rights of students. The questions in the section summarize the decisions of the Supreme Court and of lower Federal courts. School officials should consult with legal counsel in formulating their policies.

What legal standard applies to school officials who search students and their possession for drugs?

The Supreme Court has held that school officials may institute a search if there are "reasonable grounds" to believe that the search will reveal evidence that the student has violated or is violating either the law or the rules of the school.

Do School Officials Need A Search Warrant To Conduct A Search For Drugs?

No, not if they are carrying out the search independent of the police and other law enforcement officials. A more stringent legal standard may apply if enforcement officials are involved in the search.

How Extensive Can A Search Be?

The scope of the permissible search will depend on whether the measures used during the search are reasonably related to the purpose of the search and are not excessively intrusive in light of the age and sex of the student being searched. The more intrusive the search, the greater the justification that will be required by the courts.

Do School Officials Have To Stop A Search When They Find The Object Of The Search?

Not necessarily. If a search reveals items suggesting the presence of other evidence of crime or misconduct, the school officials may continue the search. For example, if a teacher is justifiably searching a student's purse for cigarettes and finds rolling papers, it will be reasonable (subject to any local policy to the contrary) for the teacher to search the rest of the purse for evidence of drugs.

Can School Officials Search Student Lockers?

Reasonable grounds to believe that a particular student locker contains evidence of a violation of the law or school rules will generally justify a search of that locker. In addition, some courts have upheld written school policies that authorize school officials to inspect student lockers it any time.

Fact Sheet; Legal Questions On Suspension And Expulsion:

The following question and answers briefly describe several federal requirements that apply to the use of suspension and expulsion as disciplinary tools in public schools. These may not reflect all laws, policies, and judicial precedents applicable to any given school district. School officials should consult with legal counsel to determine the application of these laws in their schools and to ensure compliance with all legal requirements.

What Federal Procedural Requirements Apply To Suspension Or Expulsion?

The Supreme Court has held that students facing suspension or expulsion from school are entitled under the U.S. Constitution to the basic due process protections of notice and an opportunity to be heard. The nature and formality of the "hearing" to be provided depend on the severity of the sanction being imposed.

A formal hearing is not required when a school seeks to suspend a student for 10 days or less. Due process in that situation requires only that:

A) The school inform the student, either orally or in writing of the charges and of the evidence to support those charges.

B) The school give the student an opportunity to deny the charges and present his or her side of the story.

C) As a general rule, the notice to the student and a rudimentary hearing should precede a suspension unless a student's presence poses a continuing danger to persons or property or threatens to disrupt the academic process. In such cases, the notice and rudimentary hearing should follow as soon as possible after the student's removal.

D) More formal procedures may be required for suspensions longer than 10 days and for expulsions. In addition, Federal law and regulations establish special rules governing suspensions and expulsions of students with disabilities.

E)   States and local school districts may require additional procedures.

Can Students Be Suspended Or Expelled From School For Use, Possession, Or Sale Of Drugs?

Generally, yes. A school may suspend or expel students in accordance with the terms of its discipline policy, A school policy may provide penalties of varying severity, including suspension, or expulsion, to respond to drug-related offenses. It is helpful to be explicit about the types of offenses that will be punished and about the penalties that may be imposed for particular types of offenses (e.g., use, possession, or sale of drugs). Generally, state and local law will determine the range of sanctions permitted.

D)   What Students Can Do:

1.   Learn about the effects of drug use, the reasons why drugs are harmful, and ways to resist pressures to try drugs.

2.   Use an understanding of the danger posed by drugs to help other students avoid them. Encourage other students to resist drugs, persuade those using drug to seek help, and report those selling drugs to parents and the school principal.

Learning The Facts:

Learn about the effects of alcohol and drug use, the reasons why drugs are harmful, and ways to resist pressures to try drugs. Students can arm themselves with the knowledge to resist drug use in the following ways:

1.   Learning about the effects and risk of drugs.

2.   Learning the symptoms of drug use and the names of organizations and individuals available to help when friends or family members are in trouble.

3.   Understanding the pressures to use drugs and ways to counteract them.

4.   Knowing the school rules on drugs and ways to help make the school policy work.

5.   Knowing the school procedures for reporting drug offenses.

6.   Knowing the laws on drug use and the penalties — for example, for driving under the influence of alcohol or other drugs — and, understanding how the law protects individuals and society.

7.   Developing skill in communicating their opposition to drugs and their resolve to avoid drug use.

R. H. Watkins High School of Jones County, Mississippi has developed this pledge setting forth the duties and responsibilities of student counselors in its peer counseling program.

Responsibility Pledge For A Peer Counselor R.H. Watkins High School:

As a drug education peer counselor you have the opportunity to help the youth of our community develop to their full potential without the interference of illegal drug use. It is a responsibility you must not take lightly. Therefore, please read the following responsibilities you will be expected to fulfill next school year and discuss them with your parents or guardians.

Responsibilities Of A Peer Counselor:

1. Understand and be able to clearly state your belief and attitudes about drug use among teens and adults.

2. Remain drug free.

3. Maintain an average of C or better in all classes.

4. Maintain a citizenship average of B or better.

5. Participate in some club or extracurricular activity that emphasized the positive side of school life.

6. Successfully complete training for the program, including, for example, units on the identification and symptoms of drug abuse, history and reasons for drug abuse, and the legal/economic aspects of drug abuse.

7. Successfully present monthly programs on drug abuse in each of the elementary and junior high school of the Laurel City school system, and to community groups, churches, and statewide groups as needed.

8. Participate in rap sessions or individual counseling sessions with Laurel City school students.

9. Attend at least one Jones County Drug Council meeting per year, attend the annual Drug Council Awards Banquet, work in the Drug Council Fair exhibit and in any Drug Council workshops, if needed.

10. Grades and credit for Drug Education will be awarded on successful completion of and participation in all the above-stated activities.

_____   _____
Student's Signature   Parent's or Guardian's Signature

Helping To Fight Drug Use:

Use of the understanding of the danger posed by alcohol and other drugs to help other students avoid them. Encourage other students to resist drugs, persuade those using drugs to seek help, and report those selling drugs to parents and the school principal.

Although students are the primary victims of drug use in the schools, drug use cannot be stopped or prevented unless students actively participate in this effort.

Students can help fight alcohol and other drug use in the following ways:

1. Participating in discussions about the extent of the problem at their own school.
2. Supporting a strong school anti-drug policy and firm, consistent enforcement of rules.
3. Setting a positive example for fellow students and speaking forcefully against drug use.
4. Teaching other students, particularly younger ones, about the harmful effects of drugs.
5. Encouraging their parents to join with other parents to promote a drug-free environment outside school. Some successful parent groups have been started as a result of the pressure of a son or daughter who was concerned about drugs.
6. Becoming actively involved in efforts to inform the community about the drug problem.
7. Joining in or starting a club or other activity to create positive, challenging ways for young people to have fun without alcohol other drugs. Obtaining adult sponsorship for the group and publicizing its activities.
8. Encouraging friends who have a drug problem to seek help and reporting persons selling drugs to parents and the principal.

E) What Communities Can Do:

1. Help schools fight drugs by providing them with the expertise and financial resources of community groups and agencies.
2. Involve local law enforcement agencies in all aspects of drug prevention: assessment, enforcement, and education. The police and courts should have well-established relationships with the schools,

Project DARE Los Angeles, California:

A collaborative effort begun in 1983 by the Los Angeles Police Department and the Los Angeles Unified School District, Project DARE (Drug, Abuse Resistance Education) uses uniformed law enforcement officers in classrooms as regular instructors. DARE officers use a drug curriculum that teaches students resistance to peer pressure to use drugs, self-management skills, and alternatives to *drug* use.

DARE reaches all Los Angeles Unified School District students from kindergarten through junior high school. DARE has also spread outside Los Angeles — police officers from 48 States and 1100 police agencies have received DARE training. The DARE program is also being used by the Department of Defense Dependents' Schools (military police serve as instructors).

Providing Support

In addition to providing classroom instruction, the program arranges teacher orientation, officer-student interaction (on playgrounds and in cafeterias, for example), and a parent education evening at which DARE officers explain the program to parents and provide information about symptoms of drug use and ways to increase family communication.

Studies have shown that DARE has improved students' attitudes about themselves, increase their sense of responsibility for themselves and to police, and strengthened their resistance to drugs. For example, before the DARE program began, 51 percent of fifth grade students equated drug use with having more friends. After training, only 8 percent reported this attitude.

DARE's parent program has also changed attitudes. Before DARE training, 61 percent of parents thought that there was nothing parents could do about their children's use of drugs; only 5 percent reported this opinion after the program. Before DARE training, 32 percent of parents thought that it was all right for children to drink alcohol at a party no long as adults were present. After DARE, no parents reported such a view.

Involving Law Enforcement:

Involve local law enforcement agencies in all aspects of drug prevention: assessment, enforcement, and education. The police and courts should have relationships with the schools.

Community groups can take the following actions:

1. Support school officials who take a strong position against alcohol and other drug

use.

2.   Support state and local policies to keep drugs and drug paraphernalia away from school children.

3.   Build a community consensus in favor of strong penalties for persons convicted of selling drugs, particularly for adults who have sold drugs to children.

4.   Encourage programs to provide treatment to juvenile first-offenders while maintaining tough penalties for repeat offenders and drug sellers.

Law enforcement agencies, in cooperation with schools, can take the following actions:

1.   Establish the procedure each will follow in school drug cases.

2.   Provide expert personnel to participate in prevention activities from kindergarten through grade 12.

3.   Secure areas around schools and see that the sale and use of drugs are stopped.

4.   Provide advice and personnel to help improve security in the school or on school premises.

Lincoln Junior High, Washington D.C.:

Abraham Lincoln Junior High is a modern school located in an inner-city neighborhood. Its ethnically diverse student body has 700 students, representing more than 30 countries. The student population is 51 percent Black and 43 percent Hispanic. Many of the students coming to Lincoln for the first time are newly arrived immigrants from war-torn countries.

Many of these newly arrived students are eager for acceptance by their new peers and just as eager to adjust to American culture. Teachers are keenly aware of the students' desire to fit in and realize that it is important to let these children know that the majority of American children do not use drugs nor is drug use an accepted behavior. This is not an easy task for the teachers to accomplish since the rampant drug activity going on in their neighborhood may suggest otherwise.

Lincoln's faculty-sponsored clubs are an important way teachers support what they want the drug education program to accomplish. To participate in any club, members must pledge to be drug free. Two clubs are designed to develop confidence and reinforce social and citizenship skills. Other clubs target special interests such as the Lincoln Chess

Club and LatiNero, a student arts group. A summer Substance Abuse Prevention Education Camp involves nearly 100 students in activities ranging from volleyball to dance to field trips.

The staff also encourages students to help each other. The peer Helper Club, whose members are trained in substance abuse prevention and leadership skills, publishes a handbook dispensing advice and a magazine, Cuidado Neustra Juventud (Taking Care of Our Youth), to which the entire student body can contribute.

Another innovative way the school gets its message across is by having the Student Response Team (SRT). This team is comprised of ninth graders trained to become mediators. They advertise their services within the school and get referrals from students and teachers. Students who use the services of the SRT must agree in advance to abide by the result of the mediation process or be expelled from school. Mediators meet with students in conflict at lunch or are called from class if the matter is urgent.

This multiracial team has been effective in reducing violence and convincing peers that they don't have to go to the streets to settle disputes.

F) Conclusion:

Drugs threaten our children's lives, disrupt our schools, shatter families, and, in some areas, shatter communities. Drug-related crimes overwhelm our courts, social agencies, and police. This situation need not and must not continue.

Across the United States, schools and communities have found ways to turn the tide in the battle against drugs. The methods they have used and the actions they have taken are described in this volume. We know what works; we know that drug use can be stopped.

But we cannot expect the schools to do the job without the help of parents, police, the courts, and other community groups. Drugs will be beaten only when all of us work together to deliver a firm, consistent message to those who would use or sell drugs: a message that illegal drugs will not be tolerated. It is time to join in a national effort to achieve schools without drugs.

G) Special Section:

Objective #1: To Value and Maintain Sound Personal Health; To Understand How Drugs Affect Health.

Teaching About Drug Prevention:

An effective drug prevention education program instills respect for a healthy body and mind and imparts knowledge of how the body functions, how personal habits contribute to good health, and how drugs affect the body.

At the early elementary level, children learn how to care for their bodies. Knowledge about habits, medicine, and poisons lays the foundation for learning about drugs. Older children begin to learn about the drug problem and study those drugs to which they are most likely to be exposed. The curriculum for secondary school students is increasingly drug specific as students learn about the effects of drugs on their bodies and on adolescent maturation. Health consequences of drug use, including transmission of AIDS, are emphasized.

Topics For Elementary School:

1. The roles of nutrition, medicine and health care professionals in preventing and treating disease.

2. The difficulties of recognizing which substances are safe to eat, drink, or touch; ways to learn whether a substance is safe: by consulting with an adult and by reading labels.

3. The effects of poisons on the body; the effects of medicine on the body chemistry: the wrong drug may make a person ill.

4. The nature of habits: their conscious and unconscious development.

Sample Topics For Secondary School:

1. Stress how the body responds to stress; how drugs increase stress.

2. The chemical properties of drugs.

3. The effects of drugs on the circulatory, digestive, nervous, reproductive, and respiratory systems. The effects of drugs on adolescent development

4. Patterns of substance abuse: the progressive effects of drugs on the body and mind.

5. What is addiction?

6. How to get help for a drug or alcohol problem.

Children tend to be oriented toward the present and are likely to feel invulnerable to the long-term effects of alcohol and other drugs. For this reason, they should be taught about the short-term effects of drug use (impact on appearance, alertness, and coordination) as well as about the cumulative effects.

Sample Learning Activities For Elementary School:

1. Make a coloring book depicting various substances. Color only those that are safe to eat.

2. Use puppets to dramatize what can happen when drugs are used.

3. Write stories about what to do if a stranger offers candy, pills, or a ride. Discuss options in class.

4. Try, for a time, to break a bad habit. The teacher emphasizes that it is easier not to start a bad habit than to break one.

Sample Learning Activities For Secondary School:

1. Discuss the properties of alcohol and other drugs with community experts: physicians, scientists, pharmacists, or law enforcement officers.

2. Interview social workers in drug treatment centers. Visit an open meeting of Alcoholics Anonymous or Narcotics Anonymous. These activities should be open only to mature students; careful preparation and debriefing are essential.

3. Research the drug problem at school, in the community, or in the sports and entertainment fields.

4. Design a true-false survey about drug myths and facts; conduct the survey with classmates and analyze the results.

5. Develop an accessible lending library on drugs, well stocked with up-to-date and carefully chosen materials.

When an expert visits a class, both the class and the expert should be prepared in advance. Students should learn about the expert's profession and prepare questions to ask during the visit. The expert should know what the objectives of the session are and how the session fits into previous and subsequent learning. The expert should participate in a discussion or classroom activity, not simply, appear as a speaker.

Objective #2: To respect laws and rules prohibiting drugs.

The program teaches children to respect rules and laws as the embodiment of social values and as tools for protecting individuals and society. It provides specific instruction about laws concerning drugs.

Students in the early grades learn to identify rules and to understand their importance, while older students learn about the school drug code and laws regulating drugs.

Sample Topics For Elementary School:

1. What rules are and what would happen without them.

2. What values are and why they should guide behavior.

3. What responsible behavior is.

4. Why it is wrong to take drugs.

Sample Topics For Secondary School:

1. Student responsibilities in promoting a drug-free school.

2. Local, state, and federal laws on controlled substances: why these laws exist and how they are enforced.

3. Legal consequences of drug use; penalties for driving under the influence of alcohol or drugs; the relationship between drugs and other crimes.

4. Personal and societal costs of drug use.

Sample Learning Activities For Elementary School:

1. Use stories and pictures to identify rules and laws in everyday life (e.g., lining up for recess).

2. Imagine how to get to school in the absence of traffic laws; try to play a game that has no rules.

3. Name some things that are important to adults and then list rules they have made about these things. (This activity helps explain values.)

4. Solve a simple problem (e.g., my sister hits me, or my math grades are low). Discuss which solutions are best and why.

5. Discuss school drug policies with the principal and other staff members. Learn how students can help make the policy work better.

6. Explain the connection between drug users, drug dealers, and drug traffickers and law enforcement officers whose lives are placed at risk or lost in their efforts to stop the drug trade.

Sample Learning Activities For Secondary School:

1. Resolve hypothetical school situations involving drug use. Analyze the consequences for the school, other students, and the individuals involved.

2. Collect information about accidents, crimes, and other problems related to alcohol and other drugs. Analyze how the problem might have been prevented and how the incident affected the individuals involved.

3. Conduct research projects. Interview members of the community such as attorneys, judges, police officers, state highway patrol officers, and insurance agents about the effects of alcohol and other drug use on the daily lives of teenagers and their families.

4. Draft a legislative pattern proposing enactment of a state law on drug use. Participate in a mock trail or legislative session patterned after an actual trial or debate. Through these activities, students learn to develop arguments on behalf of drug laws and their enforcement.

Objective #3: To Recognize And Resist Pressures To Use Drugs.

Social influences play a key role in encouraging children to try alcohol and other drugs. Pressures to use drugs come from internal sources, such as a child's desire to feel included in a group or to demonstrate independence, and external influences, such as the opinions and example of friends, older children and adults, and media messages.

Students must learn to identify these pressures. They must then learn how to counteract messages to use drugs and gain practice in saying no. The education program emphasizes influences on behavior, responsible decision-making, and techniques for resisting pressures to use drugs.

Sample Topics For Elementary Through High School:

1. The influence of popular cultures on behavior.

2. The influence of peers, parents, and other important individuals on a student's behavior; ways in which the need to feel accepted by others influence behavior.

3. Ways to make responsible decisions and to deal constructively with disagreeable moments and pressures.

4. Reasons for not taking drugs.

5. Situations in which students may be pressured into using alcohol and other drugs.

6. Ways of resisting pressure to use drugs.

7. Effects of drug use on family and friends, and benefits of resisting pressure to use drugs.

Sample Learning Activities For Elementary Through High School:

1. Describe recent personal decisions. In small groups, discuss what consideration influenced the decision (e.g., opinions of family or friends, beliefs, desire to be popular) and analyze choices and consequences.

2. Examine ads for cigarettes, over-the-counter drugs, and alcohol, deciding what images are being projected and whether the ads are accurate.

3. Read stories about famous people who held to their beliefs in the face of opposition. Students can discuss how these people withstood the pressure and what they accomplished.

4. Give reasons for not taking drugs. Discuss with a health educator or drug counselor the false arguments for using drugs. Develop counterarguments in response to typical messages or pressures on behalf of drug use.

5. Given a scenario depicting pressure to use drugs, act out ways of resisting (simply refusing, giving a reason, leaving the scene, etc.). Students should then practice these techniques repeatedly. Demonstrate ways of resisting pressures, using older students specially trained as peer teachers.

6. Present scenarios involving drug-related problems (e.g., learning that another student is selling drugs, learning that a sibling is using drugs, or being offered a drive home by a friend under the influence of drugs). Students practice what they would do and discuss to whom they would turn for help. Teachers should discuss and evaluate the appropriateness of student responses.

7. Discuss how it feels to resist pressures to take drugs. Hold a poster contest to depict the benefits derived both form not using and from saying no (e.g., being in control, increased respect from others, self-confidence).

Objective #4: To promote activities that reinforce the positive, drug-free elements of student life.

School activities that provide opportunities for students to have fun without alcohol and other drugs, and to contribute to the school community, build momentum for peer pressure not to use drugs. These school activities also nurture positive examples by giving older students opportunities for leadership related to drug prevention.

Sample activities:

1. Make participation in school activities dependent on an agreement not to use alco-

hol and other drugs.

2. Ensure that alcohol and other drugs will not be available at school-sponsored activities or parties. Plan these events carefully to be certain that students have attractive alternatives to drug use.

3. Give students opportunities for leadership. They can be trained to serve as peer leaders in drug prevention programs, write plays, or design posters for younger students. Activities such as these provide youthful role models who demonstrate the importance of not using drugs. Youth training programs are available that prepare students to assist in drug education and provide information on how to form drug-free youth groups.

4. Form action teams for school improvement with membership limited to students who are drug free. These action teams campaign against drug use, design special drug-free events, conduct and follow up on surveys of school needs, help teachers with paperwork, tutor other students, or improve the appearance of the school. Through these activities, students develop a stake in their school, have the opportunity to serve others, and have positive reasons to reject drug use.

5. Survey community resources that offer help for alcohol or other drug problems or ways to cope with drug use by a family member.

6. Create a program in the school for support of students returning form treatment.

How The Law Can Help:

Federal law accords school officials broad authority to regulate student conduct and supports reasonable and fair disciplinary action. In 1984, the Supreme Court reaffirmed that the constitutional rights of students in school are not "automatically coextensive with the rights of adults in other settings."

1) Rather, recognizing that "in recent years...drug use and violent crime in the schools have become major social problems," the court has emphasized the importance of effective enforcement of school rules.

2) On the whole, a school "is allowed to determine the methods of student discipline and need not exercise its discretion with undue timidity."

An effective campaign against drug use requires a basic understanding of legal techniques for searching and seizing drugs and drug-related materials, for suspending and expelling students involved with drugs and for assisting law enforcement officials in the prosecution of drug offenders. Such knowledge will help schools identify and penalize students who use or sell drugs at school and enable school officials to uncover the evidence needed to support prosecutions under Federal and State criminal laws that contain strong penalties for drug use and sale. In many cases, school officials can be instrumental in successful prosecutions.

In addition to the general Federal statutes that make it a crime to possess or distribute a controlled substance, there are special Federal laws designed to protect children and schools from drugs:

1. An important part of the Controlled Substances Act makes it a Federal crime to sell drugs in or near a public or private elementary, secondary, vocational, or postsecondary school. Under this "schoolhouse" law, sales within 1000 feet of a school are punishable by up to double the sentence that would apply if the sale occurred elsewhere. Even more serious punishments are available for repeat offenders.

2. Distribution or sale to minors of controlled substances is also a Federal crime. Then anyone age 18 or over sells drugs to anyone under 21, the seller runs the risk that he or she will receive up to double the sentence that would apply to a sell to an adult, Here too, more serious penalties can be imposed on repeat offenders.

By working with Federal and state prosecutors in their area, schools can help to ensure that these laws and others are used to make children and schools off-limits to drugs.

The following pages describe in general terms the federal laws applicable to the development of an effective school drug policy. This section is not a compendium of laws that may apply to a school district, and it is not intended to provide legal advice on all issues that may arise. School officials must recognize that many legal issues in the school context are also governed, in whole or in part, by state and local laws, which, given their diversity, cannot be covered here. Advice should be sought from legal counsel in order to understand the applicable laws and to ensure that the school's policies and actions make full use of the available methods of enforcement.

Most private schools, particularly, those that receive little or no financial assistance from public sources and are not associated with a public entity, enjoy a greater degree of legal flexibility with respect to combating the sale and use of illegal drugs.

Depending on the terms of their contracts with enrolled students, such schools may be largely free of the restrictions that normally apply to drug searches or the suspension or expulsion of student drug users. Private school officials should consult legal counsel to determine what enforcement measures may be available to them.

School procedures should reflect the available legal means for combating drug use. These procedures should be known to and understood by school administrators and teachers as well as by students, parents, and law enforcement officials. Everyone should be aware that school authorities have broad power within the law to make full, appropriate, and effective action against drug offenders,

Searching For Drugs Within The School:

In some circumstances the most important tool for controlling drug use is an effective program of drug searches. School administrators should not condone the presence of drugs anywhere on school property. The presence of any drugs or drug-related materials in school can mean only one thing — that drugs are being used or distributed in school. Schools committed to fighting drugs should do everything they can to determine whether school grounds are being used to facilitate the possession, use, or distribution of drugs, and to prevent such crimes.

To institute an effective drug search policy in schools with a substantial problem, school officials can take several steps. First, they can identify the specific areas in the school where drugs are likely to be found or used. Student lockers, bathrooms, and "smoking areas" are obvious candidates. Second, school administrators can clearly announce in writing at the beginning of the school year that these areas will be subject to unannounced searches and that students should consider such areas "public" rather than "private." The more clearly a school specifies that these portions of the school's property are public, the less likely it is that a court will conclude that students retain any reasonable expectation of privacy in these places and the less justification will be needed to search such locations.

School officials should, therefore formulate and disseminate to all students and staff a written policy that will permit an effective program of drug searches. Courts have usually upheld locker searches where schools have established written policies under which the school retains joint control over student lockers, maintains duplicate or master keys for all lockers, and reserves the right to inspect lockers at any time. Although these practices have not become established law in every part of the country, it will be easier to justify locker searches in schools that have such policies. Moreover, the mere existence of such policies can have a salutary effect. If students know that their lockers may be searched, drug users will find it much more difficult to obtain drugs in school.

The effectiveness of such searches may be improved with the use of specially trained dogs. Courts have generally held that the use of dogs to detect drugs on or in objects such as lockers, ventilators, or desks, as opposed to persons is not a "search" within the meaning of the Fourth Amendment. Accordingly, school administrators are generally justified in using dogs in this way.

It is important to remember that any illicit drugs and drug-related items discovered at school are evidence that may be used in a criminal trial. School officials should be careful, first, to protect the evidentiary integrity of such seizures by making sure that the items are obtained in permissible searches, because unlawfully acquired evidence will not be admissible in criminal proceedings. Second, school officials should work closely with local law enforcement officials to preserve, in writing, the nature and circumstances of any seizure of drug contraband. In a criminal prosecution, the State must prove that the items produced as evidence in court are the same items that were seized from the suspect. Thus, the State must establish a "chain of custody" over the seized items which accounts for the possession of the evidence from the moment of its seizure to the moment it is introduced in court. School policy regarding the disposition of drug-related items should include procedures for the custody and safekeeping of drugs and drug-related materials prior to their removal by the police and procedures for recording the circumstances regarding the seizure.

Searching Students:

In some circumstances, teachers or other school personnel will wish to search a student whom they believe to be in possession of drugs. The Supreme Court has stated that searches may be carried out according to "the dictates of reason and common sense." The court has recognized that the need of school authorities to maintain order justifies searches that might otherwise be unreasonable if undertaken by police officers or in the larger community. Thus the court has held that school officials, unlike the police, do not need "probable cause" to conduct a search, nor do they need a search warrant.

Under The Supreme Court's Rulings:

1. School officials may institute a search If there are "reasonable grounds" to believe that the search will reveal evidence that the student has violated or is violating either the law or the rules of the school.

2. The extent of the permissible search will depend on whether the measures used are reasonably related to the purpose of the search and are not excessively intrusive in light of the age and sex of the student.

3, School officials are not required to obtain search warrants when they carry out searches independent of the police and other law enforcement officials. A more stringent legal standard may apply if law enforcement officials are involved in the search.

Interpretation Of "Reasonable Grounds":

Lower courts are beginning to interpret and apply the "reasonable grounds" standard in school settings. From these cases it appears that courts will require more than general suspicion, curiosity, rumor, or a hunch to justify searching students or their possessions. Factors that will help sustain a search include the observation of specific and describable behavior or activities leading one reasonably to believe that a given student is engaging in or has engaged in prohibited conduct. The more specific the evidence in support of searching a particular student, the more likely the search will be upheld. For example, courts using a "reasonable grounds" (or similar) standard have upheld the right of school officials to search the following:

1. A student's purse, after a teacher saw her smoking in a restroom and the student denied having smoked or being a smoker.

2. A student's purse, after several other students said that she had been distributing firecrackers.

3. A student's pockets, based on a phone tip about drugs from an anonymous source believed to have previously provided accurate information.

Scope Of Permissible Search:

School officials are authorized to conduct searches within reasonable limits. The Supreme Court has described two aspects of these limits. First, when officials conduct a search, they must use only measures that are reasonably related to the purpose of the search. Second, the search may not be excessively intrusive in light of the age or sex of the student. For example, if a teacher believes he or she has seen one student passing a marijuana cigarette to another student, the teacher might reasonably search the students and any nearby belongings in which the students might have tried to hide the drug. If it turns out that what the teacher saw was a stick of gum, the teacher would have no justification for any further search for drugs.

The more intrusive the search, the greater the justification that will be required by the courts. A search of a student's jacket or bookbag can often be justified as reasonable. At the other end of the spectrum, strip searches are considered a highly intrusive invasion of individual privacy and are viewed with disfavor by the courts (although even these searches have been upheld in certain extraordinary circumstances).

School officials do not necessarily have to stop a search if they find what they are looking for. If the search of a student reveals items that create reasonable grounds for suspecting that the student may also possess other evidence of crime or misconduct, the school officials may continue the search. For example, if a teacher justifiably searches a student's purse for cigarettes and finds rolling papers like those used for marijuana cigarettes, it will then be reasonable for the teacher to search the rest of the purse for other evidence of drugs.

Consent:

If a student consents to a search, the search is permissible, regardless of whether there would otherwise be reasonable grounds for the search. To render such a search valid, however, the student must give consent knowingly and voluntarily.

Establishing whether the student's consent was voluntary can be difficult, and the burden is on the school officials to prove voluntary consent. If a student agrees to be searched out of fear or as a result of other coercion, that consent will probably be found invalid. Similarly, if school officials indicate that a student must agree to a search or if the student is very young or otherwise unaware that he or she has the right to object, the student's consent will also be held invalid. School officials may find it helpful to explain to students that they do not have to consent to a search. In some cases, standard consent forms may be useful.

If a student is asked to consent to a search and refuses, that refusal does not mean that the search may not be conducted, Rather, in the absence of consent, school officials retain the authority to conduct a search when there are reasonable grounds to justify it, as described previously.

Special Types Of Student Searches:

Schools with severe drug problems may occasionally wish to resort to more intrusive searches, such as the use of trained dogs or urinalysis, to screen students for drug use. The Supreme Court has yet to address these issues. The following paragraphs explain the existing rulings on these subjects by other courts:

1. Specially trained dogs. The few courts that have considered this issue disagree as to whether the use of a specially trained dog to detect drugs on students constitutes a search within the meaning of the Fourth Amendment. Some courts have held that a dog's sniffing of a student is a search, and that, in the school setting, individualized grounds for reasonable suspicion are required in order for such a "sniff-search" to be held constitutional. Under this standard, a blanket search of a school's entire student population by specially trained dogs would be prohibited.

   At least one other court has held that the use of trained dogs does, not constitute a search, and has permitted the use of such dogs without individualized grounds for suspicion. Another factor that courts may consider is the way that the dogs detect the presence of drugs. In some instances, the dogs are merely led down hallways or classroom aisles. In contrast, having the dogs actually touch parts of the students' bodies is more intrusive and would probably require specific justification.

   Courts have generally held that the use of specially trained dogs to detect drugs on objects, as opposed to persons, is not a search within the meaning of the Fourth Amendment. Therefore, school officials may often be able to use dogs to inspect student lockers and school property.

2. Drug testing, the use of urinalysis or other tests to screen students for drugs is a relatively new phenomenon and the law in this area is still evolving. Few courts have considered the use of urinalysis to screen public school students for drugs, and those courts that have done so have reached mixed results. The permissibility of drug testing of students has not been determined under all circumstances, although drug testing of adults has been upheld in some settings.

Suspension And Expulsion:

A school policy may lawfully provide for penalties of varying severity, including suspension and expulsion, to respond to drug-related offenses. The Supreme Court has held that because schools "need to be able to impose disciplinary sanctions for a wide range of unanticipated conduct disruptive of the educational process." a school's disciplinary rules need not be so, detailed as criminal code. Nonetheless, it is helpful for school policies to be explicit about the types of offenses that will be punished and about the penalties that may be imposed for each of these (e.g., use, possession, or sale of drugs). State and local law will usually determine the range of sanctions that is permissible. In general, courts will require only that the penalty imposed for drug-related misconduct be rationally related to the severity of the offense.

School officials should not forget that they have jurisdiction to impose punishment for some drug-related offenses that occur off-campus. Depending on state and local laws, schools are often able to punish conduct at off-campus, school-sponsored events as well as off-campus conduct that has a direct and immediate effect on school activities.

Procedural Guidelines:

Students facing suspension or expulsion from school are entitled under the U.S. Constitution and most State constitutions to common sense due process protections of notice and an opportunity to be heard. Because the Supreme Court has recognized that a school's ability to maintain order would be impeded if formal procedures were required every time school authorities sought to discipline a student, the court has held that the nature and formality of the "hearing" will depend on the severity of the sanction being imposed.

A formal hearing is not required when a school seeks to suspend a student for 10 days or less. The Supreme Court has held that due process in that situation requires only that:

1. The school must inform the student, either orally or in writing, of the charges against him or her and of the evidence to support those charges.

2. The school must give the student an opportunity to deny the charges and present his or her side of the story.

3. As a general rule, this notice and rudimentary hearing should precede a suspension. However, a student whose presence poses a continuing danger to persons or property or an ongoing threat of disrupting the academic process may be immediately removed from school. In such a situation, the notice and rudimentary hearing should

follow as soon as possible.

The Supreme Court has also stated that more formal procedures may be required for suspensions longer than 10 days and for expulsions. Although the Court has not established specific procedures to be followed in those situations, other Federal courts have set the following guidelines for expulsions. These guidelines would apply to suspensions longer than 10 days as well:

1. The student must be notified in writing of the specific charges against him or her, which, if proven, would justify expulsion.

2. The student should be given the names of the witnesses against him or her and an oral or written report on the facts to which each witness will testify.

3. The student should be given the opportunity to present a defense against the charges and to produce witnesses or testimony on his or her behalf.

Many states have laws governing the procedures required for suspensions and expulsions. Because applicable statutes and judicial rulings vary across the country, local school districts may enjoy a greater or lesser degree of flexibility in establishing procedures for suspensions and expulsions.

School officials must also be aware of the special procedures that apply to suspension or expulsion of students with disabilities under Federal law and regulations.

Effects Of Criminal Proceedings Against A Student:

A school may usually pursue disciplinary action against a student regardless of the status of any outside criminal prosecution. That is Federal law does not require the school to await the outcome of the criminal prosecution before initiating proceedings to suspend or expel a student or to impose whatever other penalty is appropriate for the violation of the school's rules. In addition, a school is generally free under Federal law to discipline a student when there is evidence that the student has violated a school rule, even if a juvenile court has acquitted (or convicted) the student or if local authorities have declined to prosecute criminal charges stemming from the same incident. Schools may wish to discuss this subject with counsel.

Effect Of Expulsion:

State and local law will determine the effect of expelling a student from school. Some state laws require the provision of alternative schooling for students below a certain age. In other areas, expulsion may mean the removal from public schools for the balance of the school year or even the permanent denial of access to the public school system.

Confidentiality Of Education Records:

To rid their schools of drugs, school officials will periodically need to report drug-related crimes to police and to help local law enforcement authorities detect and prosecute drug offenders. In doing so, schools will need to take steps to ensure compliance with Federal and State laws governing confidentiality of student records.

The Federal law that addresses this issue is the Family Educational Rights and Privacy Act (FERPA), which applies to any school that receives Federal funding and which limits the disclosure of certain information about students that is contained in education records. Under FERPA, disclosure of information in education records to individuals or entities other than parents, students and school officials is permissible only in specified situations. In many cases, unless the parents or an eligible student provides written consent, FERPA will limit a school's ability to turn over education records or to disclose information from them to the police. Such disclosure is permitted, however, if 1) it is required by a court order or subpoena, or 2) it is warranted by a health and safety emergency. In the first of these two cases, reasonable efforts must be made to notify the student's parents before the disclosure is made. FERPA also permits disclosure if a State law enacted before November 19, 1974, specifically requires disclosure to State and local officials.

Schools should be aware, however, that because FERPA governs only the information in education records, it does not limit disclosure of other information. Thus, school employees are free to disclose any information of which they become aware through personal observation. For example, a teacher who witnesses a drug transaction may, when the police arrive, report what he or she witnessed. Similarly, evidence seized from a student during a search is not an education record and may not be turned over to the police without constraint,

State laws and school policies may impose additional, and sometimes more restrictive, requirements regarding the disclosure of information about students. Because this area of the law is complicated, it is especially important that an attorney be involved in formulating school policy under FERPA and applicable State laws.

Other Legal Issues; Lawsuits Against Schools Or School Officials:

Disagreements between parents or students and school officials about disciplinary measures usually can be resolved informally. Occasionally, however, a school's decisions and activities relating to disciplinary matters are the subject of lawsuits by parents or students against administrators, teachers, and school systems. For these reasons, it is advisable that school districts obtain adequate insurance coverage for themselves and for all school personnel for liability arising from disciplinary actions.

Suits may be brought in Federal or State court; typically, they are based on a claim that a student's constitutional or statutory rights have been violated. Frequently, these suits will seek to revoke the school district's imposition of some disciplinary measure, for example, by ordering the reinstatement of a student who has been expelled or suspended. Suits may also attempt to recover money damages from the school district or the employee involved, or both; however, court awards of money damages are extremely rare. Moreover, although there can be no guarantee of a given result in any particular case, courts in recent years have tended to discourage such litigation.

In general, disciplinary measures imposed reasonably and in accordance with established legal requirements will be upheld by the courts. As a rule, Federal judges will not substitute their interpretations of school rules, or regulations for those of local school authorities, or otherwise second-guess reasonable decisions by school officials. In addition, school officials are entitled to qualified good-faith immunity from personal liability for having violated a student's Federal constitutional or civil rights. When this immunity applies, it shields school officials from any personal liability for money damages. Thus, as a general matter, personal liability is very rare, because officials should not be held personally liable unless their actions are clearly unlawful, unreasonable, or arbitrary.

When a court does award damages, the award may be "compensatory" or "punitive." Compensatory damages are awarded to compensate, the student for injuries actually suffered as a result of the violation of his or her rights and cannot be based upon the abstract "value" or "importance" of the constitutional rights in question. The burden is on the student to prove that he or she suffered actual injury as a result of the deprivation. Thus, a student who is suspended, but not under the required procedures, will not be entitled to compensation if the student would have been suspended had a proper hearing been held. If the student cannot prove that the failure to hold a hearing itself caused him or her some compensable harm, then the student is entitled to no more than nominal damages, such as $1.00. "Punitive damages" are awarded to punish the perpetrator of the injury. Normally, punitive damages are awarded only when the conduct in question is malicious, unusually reckless, or otherwise reprehensible.

Parents and students can also claim that actions by a school or school officials have violated State law. For example, it can be asserted that a teacher "assaulted" a student in violation of a State criminal law. The procedures and standards in actions involving such violations are determined by each state. Some States provide a qualified immunity from tort liability under standards similar to the "good faith" immunity in Federal civil rights actions. Other States provide absolute immunity under their law for actions taken in the course of a school official's duties.

Nondiscrimination In Enforcement Of Discipline:

Federal law applicable to programs or activities receiving Federal financial assistance prohibits school officials who are administering discipline from discriminating against students on the basis of race, color, national origin, or sex. Schools should therefore administer their discipline policies evenhandedly, without regard to such considerations. Thus, as a general matter, students with similar disciplinary records who violate the same rule in the same way should be treated similarly. For example, it male and female students with no prior record of misbehavior are caught together smoking marijuana, it would not, in the absence of other relevant factors, be advisable for the school to suspend the male student for 10 days while imposing only an afternoon detention on the female student. Such divergent penalties for the same offense may be appropriate, however, if the student who received the harsher punishment had a history of misconduct or committed other infractions after this first confrontation with school authorities.

School officials should also be aware of and adhere to the special rules and procedures for the disciplining of students with disabilities under the Individuals with Disabilities Education Act, 20 U.S.C. 140020 and Section 504 of the Rehabilitation Act of 1973, 29 U.S.C. 794.

Resources

Specific Drugs And Their Effects:

Tobacco (Effects)

The smoking of tobacco products is the chief avoidable cause of death in our society. Smokers are more likely than nonsmokers to contract heart disease — some 170,000 die each year from smoking-related coronary heart disease. Lung, larynx, esophageal, bladder, pancreatic, and kidney cancers also strike smokers at increased rates. Some 30 percent of cancer deaths (130,000 per year) are linked to smoking. Chronic obstructive lung diseases such as emphysema and chronic bronchitis are 10 times more likely to occur among smokers than among nonsmokers.

Smoking during pregnancy also poses serious risks. Spontaneous abortion, pre-term birth, low birth weights, and fetal and infant deaths are all more likely to occur when the pregnant woman/mother is a smoker.

Cigarette smoke contains some 4,000 chemicals, several of which are known carcinogens. Other toxins and irritants found in smoke can produce eye, nose, and throat irritations. Carbon monoxide, another component of cigarette smoke, combines with hemoglobin in the blood stream to form carboxyhemoglobin, a substance that interferes with the body's ability to obtain and use oxygen.

Perhaps the most dangerous substance in tobacco smoke is nicotine. Although it is implicated in the onset of heart attacks and cancer, its most dangerous role is reinforcing and strengthening the desire to smoke. Because nicotine is highly addictive, addicts find it very difficult to stop smoking. Of 1,000 typical smokers, fewer than 20 percent succeed in stopping on the first try.

Although the harmful effects of smoking cannot be questioned, people who quit can make significant strides in repairing damage done by smoking. For pack-a-day smokers, the increased risk of heart attack dissipates after 10 years. The likelihood of contracting lung cancer as a result of smoking can also be greatly reduced by quitting.

Alcohol (Effects):

Alcohol consumption causes a number of marked changes in behavior. Even low doses significantly impair the judgment and coordination required to drive a car safely, increasing the likelihood that the driver will be involved in an accident. Low to moderate doses of alcohol also increase the incidence of a variety of aggressive acts, including spouse and child abuse. Moderate to high doses of alcohol cause marked impairments in higher mental functions, severely altering a person's ability to learn and remember information. Very high doses cause respiratory depression and death. If combined with other depressants of the central nervous system, much lower doses of alcohol will produce the effects just described.

Repeated use of alcohol can lead to dependence. Sudden cessation of alcohol intake is likely to produce withdrawal symptoms, including severe anxiety, tremors, hallucinations, and convulsions. Alcohol withdrawal can be life threatening. Long-term consumption of large quantities of alcohol, particularly when combined with poor nutrition, can also lead to permanent damage to vital organs such as the brain and liver.

Mothers who drink alcohol during pregnancy may give birth to infants with fetal alcohol syndrome. These infants have irreversible physical abnormalities and mental retardation. In addition, research indicates that children of alcoholic parents are at greater risk than other youngsters of becoming alcoholics.

Cannabis (Effects):

All forms of cannabis have negative physical and mental effects. Several regularly observed physical effects of cannabis are a substantial increase in the heart rate, bloodshot eyes, a dry mouth and throat, and increased appetite.

Use of cannabis may impair or reduce short-term memory and comprehension, alter sense of time, and reduce ability to perform tasks requiring concentration and coordination, such as driving a car.

Research also shows that students do not retain knowledge when they are "high." Motivation and cognition may be altered, making the acquisition of new information difficult. Marijuana can also produce paranoia and psychosis.

Because users often inhale the unfiltered smoke deeply and then hold it in their lungs as long as possible, marijuana is damaging to the lungs and pulmonary system. Marijuana smoke contains more cancer-causing agents than tobacco smoke.

Long-term users of cannabis may develop psychological dependence and require more of the drug to get the same effect. The drug can become the center of their lives.

Inhalants (Effects):

The immediate negative effects of inhalants include nausea, sneezing, coughing, nosebleeds, fatigue, lack of coordination, and loss of appetite. Solvents and aerosol sprays also decrease the heart and respiratory rates and impair judgment. Amyl and butyl nitrite cause rapid pulse, headaches, and involuntary passing of urine and feces. Long-term use may result in hepatitis or brain damage.

Deeply inhaling the vapors, or using large amounts over a short time may result in disorientation, violent behavior, unconsciousness, or death. High concentrations of inhalants can cause suffocation by displacing the oxygen in the lungs or by depressing the central nervous system to the point that breathing stops.

Long-term use can cause weight loss, fatigue, electrolyte imbalance, and muscle fatigue. Repeated sniffing of concentrated vapors over time can permanently damage the nervous system.

Cocaine (Effects):

Cocaine stimulates the central nervous system. Its immediate effects include dilated pupils and elevated blood pressure, heart rate, respiratory rate, and body temperature. Occasional use can cause a stuffy or runny nose, while chronic use can ulcerate the mucous membrane of the nose. Injecting cocaine with contaminated equipment can cause AIDS, hepatitis, and other diseases. Preparation of freebase, which involves the use of volatile solvents, can result in death or injury from fire or explosion. Cocaine can produce psychological and physical dependency, a feeling that the user cannot function without the drug. In addition, tolerance develops rapidly.

Crack or freebase rock is extremely addictive, and its effects are felt within 10 seconds. The physical effects include dilated pupils, increased pulse rate, elevated blood pressure, insomnia, loss of appetite, tactile hallucinations, paranoia, and seizures. The use of cocaine can cause death by cardiac arrest or respiratory failure.

Other Stimulants (Effects):

Stimulants can cause increased heart and respiratory rates, elevated blood pressure, dilated pupils, and decreased appetite. In addition, users may experience sweating, headache, blurred vision, dizziness, sleeplessness, and anxiety. Extremely high doses can cause a rapid or irregular heartbeat, tremors, loss of coordination, and even physical collapse. An amphetamine injection creates a sudden increase in blood pressure that can result in stroke, very high fever, or heart failure.

In addition to the physical effects, users report feeling restless, anxious, and moody. Higher doses intensify the effects. Persons who use large amounts of amphetamines over a long period of time can develop an amphetamine psychosis that include halluci-nations, delusions, and paranoia. These symptoms usually disappear when the drug use ceases.

Depressants (Effects):

The effects of depressants are in many ways similar to the effects of alcohol. Small amounts can produce calmness and relaxed muscles, but somewhat larger doses can cause slurred speech, staggering gait, and altered perception. Very large doses can cause res-piratory depression, coma, and death. The combination of depressants and alcohol can multiply the effects of the drugs, thereby multiplying the risk.

The use of depressants can cause both physical and psychological dependence. Regu-lar use over time may result in a tolerance to the drug, leading the user to increase the quantity consumed. When regular users suddenly stop taking large doses, they may de-velop withdrawal symptoms ranging from restlessness, insomnia, and anxiety to convul-sions and death.

Babies born to mothers who abuse depressants during pregnancy may be physically dependent on the drugs and show withdrawal symptoms shortly after they are born. Birth defects and behavioral problems also may result.

Hallucinogens (Effects):

Phencyclidine (PCP) interrupts the functions of the neocortex, the section of the brain that controls the intellect and keeps instincts in check. Because the drug blocks pain receptors, violent PCP episodes may result in self-inflicted injuries.

The effects of PCP vary, but users frequently report a sense of distance and estrange-ment. Time and body movement are slowed down. Muscular coordination worsens and senses are dulled. Speech is blocked and incoherent.

Chronic users of PCP report persistent memory problems and speech difficulties. Some of theses effects may last 6 months to a year following prolonged daily use. Mood disorders — depression, anxiety, and violent behavior — also occur. In later stages of chronic use, users often exhibit paranoid and violent behavior and experience hallu-cinations.

Large doses may produce convulsions and coma, as well as heart and lung failure.

Lysergic acid (LSD), mescaline, and psilocybin cause illusions and hallucinations. The physical effects may include dilated pupils, elevated body temperature, increased heart rate and blood pressure, loss of appetite, sleeplessness, and tremors.

Sensations and feelings may change rapidly. It is common to have a bad psychological reaction to LSD, mescaline, and psilocybin. The user may experience panic, confusion, suspicion, anxiety, and loss of control. Delayed effects, or flashbacks, can occur even after use has ceased.

Narcotics (Effects):

Narcotics initially produce a feeling of euphoria that often is followed by drowsiness, nausea, and vomiting. Users also may experience constricted pupils, watery eyes, and itching. An overdose may produce slow and shallow breathing, clammy skin, convulsions, coma, and possible death.

Tolerance to narcotics develops rapidly and dependence is likely. The use of contaminated syringes may result in disease such as AIDS, endocarditis, and hepatitis. Addiction in pregnant women can lead to premature, stillborn, or addicted infants who experience severe withdrawal symptoms.

Designer Drugs (Effects):

Illegal drugs are defined in terms of their chemical formulas. To circumvent these legal restrictions, underground chemists modify the molecular structure of certain illegal drugs to produce analogs known as designer drugs. These drugs can be several hundred times stronger than the drugs they are designed to imitate.

Many of the so-called designer drugs are related to amphetamines and have mild stimulant properties but are mostly euphoriants. They can produce severe neurochemical damage to the brain.

The narcotic analogs can cause symptoms such as those seen in Parkinson's disease: uncontrollable tremors, drooling, impaired speech, paralysis, and irreversible brain damage. Analogs of amphetamines and methamphetamines cause nausea, blurred vision, chills or sweating, and faintness. Psychological effects include anxiety, depression, and paranoia. As little as one dose can cause brain damage. The analogs of phencyclidine cause illusions, hallucinations, and impaired perception.

Anabolic Steroids:

Anabolic steroids are a group of powerful compounds closely related to the male sex hormone testosterone. Developed in the 1930s, steroids are seldom prescribed by physicians today. Current legitimate medical uses are limited to certain kinds of anemia, severe burns, and some types of breast cancer.

Taken in combination with a program of muscle-building exercise and diet, steroids may contribute to increases in body weight and muscular strength. Because of these properties, athletes in a variety of sports have used steroids since the 1950s, hoping to enhance performance. Today, they are being joined by increasing numbers of young people seeking to accelerate their physical development.

Steroid users subject themselves to more than 70 side effects ranging in severity from liver cancer to acne and including psychological as well as physical reactions. The liver and the cardiovascular and reproductive systems are most seriously affected by steroid use. In males, use can cause withered testicles, sterility, and impotence. In females, irreversible masculine traits can develop along with breast reduction and sterility. Psychological effects in both sexes include very aggressive behavior known as "road rage" and depression. While some side effects appear quickly, others, such as heart attacks and strokes, may not show up for years.

Signs of steroid use include quick weight and muscle gains (if steroids are being used in conjunction with a weight training program; behavioral changes, particularly increased aggressiveness and combativeness; jaundice; purple or red spots on the body; swelling of feet or lower legs; trembling; unexplained darkening of the skin; persistent unpleasant breath odor, and severe acne.

Steroids are produced in tablet or capsule form for oral ingestion, or as a liquid for intramuscular injection.

Sources Of Information:
Toll-Free Information:
1-800-COCAINE — Cocaine Helpline

A round-the-clock information and referral service. Recovering cocaine addict counselors answer the phones, offer guidance, and refer drug users and parents to local public and private treatment centers and family learning centers.

1-800-NCA-CALL — National Council On Alcoholism Information Line

The National Council on Alcoholism, Inc., is the national nonprofit organization combating alcoholism, other drug additions, and related problems. Provides information about NCA's State and local affiliates' activities in their areas. Also provides referral services to families and individuals seeking help with an alcohol or other drug problem.

1-800-662-HELP — NIDA Hotline

NIDA Hotline, operated by the National Institute on Drug Abuse, is a confidential information and referral line that directs callers to cocaine abuse treatment centers in the local community. Free materials on drug use also are distributed in response to inquiries.

General Readings:

Publications listed below are free unless otherwise noted.

Adolescent Drug Abuse: Analyses of Treatment Research, by Elizabeth R. Rahdert and John Grabowski, 1988. This 139-page book assesses the adolescent drug user and offers theories, techniques, and findings about treatment and prevention. It also discusses family based approaches. National Clearinghouse for Alcohol and Drug Information, P.O. Box 2345, Rockville, MD 20852.

Adolescent Peer Pressure Theory, Correlates, and Program Implications for Drug Abuse Prevention, 1988, U.S. Department of Health and Human Services. This 115-page book focuses on constructive ways of channeling peer pressure. This volume was developed to help parents and professionals understand the pressures associated with adolescence, the factors associated with drug use, and other forms of problem behavior. Different peer program approaches, ways in which peer programs can be implemented, and research suggestions are included. National Clearinghouse for Alcohol and Drug Information, P.O. Box 2343, Rockville, MD 20852.

Building Drug-Free Schools, by Richard A. Hawley, Robert C. Peterson, and Margaret C. Mason, 1986. This four-part drug prevention kit for grades K-12 provides school staff, parents, and community groups with suggestions for developing a workable school policy, K-12 curriculum, and community support. The kit consists of three written guides ($50) and a film ($275). American Council for Drug Education, 204 Monroe Street, Suite 110, Rockville, MD 20852. Telephone (301) 294-0600.

The Challenge newsletter highlights successful school-based programs, provides suggestions on effect prevention techniques and the latest research on drugs and their effects. Published quarterly by the U.S. Department of Education and available from the National Clearinghouse for Alcohol and Drug Information, P.O. Box 2345, Rockville,

MD 20852.

Courtwatch Manual. An 111-page manual explaining the court system, the criminal justice process, Courtwatch activities, and what can be done before and after a criminal is sentenced. Washington Legal Foundation, 1705 N. Street, NW, Washington, DC 20036. Enclose $5 for postage and handling. Telephone (202) 857-0240.

Drug Prevention Curricula: A Guide to Selection and Implementation, by the U.S. Department of Education, 1988. Written with the help of a distinguished advisory panel, this 76-page handbook represents the best current thinking about drug prevention education. It shows what to look for when adopting ready-made curricula, and suggests important lessons that ought to be part of any prevention education sequence. National Clearinghouse for Alcohol and Drug Information, P.O. Box 2345, Rockville, MD 20852.

Getting Tough on Gateway Drugs, by Robert DuPont, Jr., 1985. This 330-page book describes the drug problem, the drug-dependence syndrome, the gateway drugs, and some ways that families can prevent and treat drug problems. American Psychiatric Press, Inc., 1400 K. Street, NW, Suite 1101, Washington, DC 20005, paperback, $9.95. Telephone (800) 368-5777 and in the DC area (202) 682-6269.

Gone Way Down: Teenage Drug-Use Is a Disease, by Miller Newton, 1981, revised 1987. This 72-page book describes the stages of adolescent drug use. American Studies Press, paperback, $3.95. Telephone (813) 961-7200.

Kids and Drugs: A Handbook for Parents and Professionals, by Joyce Tobias, 1986, reprinted 1987. A 96-page handbook about adolescent drug and alcohol use, the effects of drugs and the drug culture, stages of chemical use, the formation of parent groups, and available resources. PANDAA Press, 4111 Watkins Trail, Annandale, VA. 22003. Telephone (703) 750-9285, paperback, $4.95 (volume discounts).

National Trends in Drug Use and Related Factors Among American High School Students, 1975-1986, by Jerald G. Bachman, Lloyd D. Johnston, and Patrick M. O'Malley, 1987. This 265-page book reports on trends in drug use and attitudes of high school seniors, based on an annual survey conducted since 1975. National Clearinghouse for Alcohol and Drug Information, P.O. Box 2343, Rockville, MD 20852.

Parents, Peers and Pot 2: Parents in Action, by Marsha Manatt, 1983, reprinted 1988. This 160-page book describes the information of parent groups in rural, suburban, and urban communities. National Clearinghouse for Alcohol and Drug Information, P.O. Box 2345, Rockville, MD 20852.

Peer Pressure Reversal, by Sharon Scott, 1985, reprinted 1988. A 183-page guidebook for parents, teachers, and concerned citizens to enable them to teach peer pressure reversal skills to children. Human Resource Development Press, 22 Amherst Road, Amherst, MA 01002. Telephone (413) 253-3488, paperback, $9.95.

Pot Safari, by Peggy Mann, 1982, reprinted 1987. A 134-page book for parents and teenagers. Distinguished research scientists are interviewed on the subject of marijuana. Woodmere Press, Cathedral Finance Station, P.O. Box 20190, New York, NY 10125. Telephone (212) 678-7839. Paperback, $6.95 plus shipping (volume discounts).

Strategies for Controlling Adolescent Drug Use, by Michael J. Polich et al., 1984. This 196-page book reviews the scientific literature on the nature of drug use and the effectiveness of drug law enforcement, treatment, and prevention programs. The Rand Corporation, 1700 Main Street, P.O. Box 2138, Santa Monica, California 90406-2138, R-3076-CHF. Telephone (213) 393-0411, paperback $15.00.

Team Up for Drug Prevention With America's Young Athletes. A free booklet for coaches that includes information about alcohol and other drugs, reasons why athletes use drugs, suggested activities for coaches, a prevention program, a survey for athletes and coaches, and sample letters to parents. Drug Enforcement Administration, Demand Reduction Section, 1405 I Street, NW, Washington, DC 20537 Telephone (202) 786-4096.

The Fact Is ... You Can Prevent Alcohol and Other Drug Problems Among Elementary School Children, 1988. This 17-page booklet includes audiovisuals program descriptions and professional and organizational resources to assist educators and parents of young children. National Clearinghouse for Alcohol and Drug Information, P.O. Box 2345, Rockville, MD 20852.

Videotapes:

The following drug prevention videos were developed by the U.S. Department of Education. They are Available for loan through the Department's Regional Centers and the National Clearinghouse for Alcohol and Drug Information, P.O. Box 2345, Rockville, MD 20852; (301) 468-2600.

Elementary School:

The Drug Avengers. Ten 5-minute animated adventures that urge caution about ingesting unfamiliar substances; encourage students to trust their instincts when they think something is wrong; and show that drugs make things worse, not better.

Fast Forward Future. A magical device allows youngsters to peer into the future and see on a TV screen what will happen if they use drugs and what will happen if they remain drug free.

Straight Up. A fantasy adventure that features information on the effects of drugs, developing refusal skills, building self-esteem, and resisting peer pressure.

Junior High:

Straight at Ya. Tips on peer pressure, saying no and building self-esteem.

Lookin' Good. A two part series based on actual incidents that convey the dangers of drug use and promote the use of peer support groups.

Straight Talk. Teens discuss why they won't use drugs and ways to avoid drugs.

High School:

Hard Facts About Alcohol, Marijuana, and Crack. Offers factual information about the dangers of drug use in a series of dramatic vignettes.

Speak Up, Speak Out: Learning To Say No To Drugs. Gives students specific techniques they can use to resist peer pressure and say no to drug use.

Dare to Be Different. Uses the friendship of two athletes in their last year of high school to illustrate the importance of goals and values in resisting pressures to use drugs.

Downfall: Sports and Drugs. Shows how drugs affect athletic performance and examines the consequences of drug use, including steroid use, on every aspect of an athlete's life — career, family, friends, sense of accomplishment, and self-esteem.

Private Victories. Illustrates the effects of drug and alcohol use on students and the value of positive peer influences in resisting peer pressure to use drugs.

Sources Of Free Catalogs Of Publications:

Hazeld Education Materials. A source for pamphlets and books on drug use and alcoholism and curriculum materials for drug prevention. Telephone (800) 328-9000. In Minnesota, call (612) 257-4010 or (800) 257-0070.

National Council on Alcoholism. A source for pamphlets, booklets, and fact sheets on alcoholism and drug use. Telephone (212) 206-6770.

Johnson Institute. A source for audiocassettes, films, videocassettes, pamphlets, and books on alcoholism and drug use. Offers books and pamphlets on prevention and intervention for children, teens, parents, and teachers. Telephone Toll Free (800) 247-0484 and in Minneapolis/St. Paul area, 944-0511.

National Association for Children of Alcoholics. A source for books, pamphlets, and handbooks for children of alcoholics. Conducts regional workshops and provides a directory of local members and meetings. Telephones (714) 499-3889.

School And Community Resources:

ACTION Drug Prevention Program. ACTION, the Federal volunteer agency, works at the local, state, and national levels to encourage and help fund the growth of youth, parents, and senior citizen groups and networks committed to helping youth remain drug free. 806 Connecticut Avenue, NW, Suite M-606, Washington, DC 20525. Telephone (202) 634-9757.

American Council for Drug Education (ACDE). ACDE organizes conferences; develops media campaigns; reviews scientific findings; publishes books, a quarterly newsletter, and education kits for physicians, schools, and libraries; and produces films. 204 Monroe Street, Suite 110, Rockville, MD 20852. Telephone (301) 294-0600.

Committees of Correspondence. This organization provides a newsletter and bulletins on issues, ideas, and contracts. Publishes a resource list and pamphlets. Membership is $15.00. 57 Conant Street, Room 113, Danvers, MA 09123. Telephone (508) 774-2641.

Drug-Free Schools and Communities—Regional Centers Program, U.S. Department of Education. This program is designed to help local school districts, state education agencies, and institutions of higher education to develop alcohol and drug education and prevention programs. Five regional centers provide training and technical assistance. For further information on center services, contact the center in your region:

Northeast Regional Center for Drug-free Schools and Communities
12 Overton Ave.
Sayville, NY 11782-0403
(516) 589-7022

Connecticut, Delaware, Maine, Maryland, Massachusetts, New Hampshire, New Jersey, New York, Ohio, Pennsylvania, Rhode Island, Vermont

Southeast Regional Center for Drug-Free Schools and Communities Spencerian Office Plaza
University of Louisville
Louisville, Ky 40292
(502) 588-0052
FAX: (502) 588-1782

Alabama, District of Columbia, Florida, Georgia, Kentucky, North Carolina, Puerto Rico, South Carolina, Tennessee, Virginia, Virgin Islands, West Virginia

Midwest Regional Center for Drug-Free Schools and Communities
1900 Spring Road
Oak Brook, IL 60521
(708) 571-4710 Fax: (708) 571-4718

Indiana, Illinois, Iowa, Michigan, Minnesota, Missouri, Nebraska, North Dakota, South Dakota, Wisconsin

Southwest Regional Center for Drug-free Schools and Communities 555 Constitution Ave.
Norman, OK 73037-0005
(405) 325-1454
(800) 234-7972 (outside Oklahoma)

Arizona, Arkansas, Colorado, Kansas, Louisiana, Mississippi, New Mexico, Oklahoma, Texas, Utah

Western Regional Center for Drug-Free Schools and Communities
101 S.W. Main St., Suite 500
Portland, OR 97204
(800) 547-6339 (outside Oregon)

Alaska, California, Hawaii, Idaho, Montana, Nevada, Oregon, Washington, Wyoming, American Samoa, Guam, and Republic of Palau

For general program information, contact the U.S. Department of Education Drug-Free School Staff, 400 Maryland Avenue, SW, Washington, DC 20202-6151. Telephone (202) 732-4599.

Drug-Free Schools and Communities—State and Local programs, U.S. Department of Education. This program provides each State Educational agency and Governor's Office with funds for alcohol and drug education and prevention programs in local schools and communities. For information on contact persons in your state, contact the U.S. Department of Education, Drug-Free Schools Staff, 400 Maryland Avenue, SW, Washington, DC 20202-5151. Telephone (202) 732-4599.

Families in Action. This organization maintains a drug information center with more than 200,000 documents. Publishes Drug Abuse Update, a quarterly journal containing abstracts of articles published in medical and academic journals and newspapers. $25 for four issues. 2296 Henderson Mill Road, Suite 204, Atlanta, GA 30345. Telephone (404) 934-6364.

"Just Say No" Clubs. These nationwide clubs provide support and positive peer reinforcement to youngsters through workshops, seminars, newsletters, walk-a-thons, and a variety of other activities. Clubs are organized by schools, communities, and parent groups. Just Say No Foundation, 1777 N. California Boulevard, Suite 200, Walnut Creek, CA 94596. Telephone (800) 258-2766 or (415) 939-6666.

Narcotics Education, Inc. The organization publishes pamphlets, books, teaching aids, posters, audiovisual aids, and prevention magazines designed for classroom use: WINNER for Preteens and LISTEN for teens. 6830 Laurel Street, NW, Washington, DC 20012. Telephone (800) 548-8700, or in the Washington, DC area, (202) 722-6740.

Parents' Resource Institute for Drug Education, Inc. (PRIDE). This national resource and information center offers consultant services to parent groups, school personnel, and youth groups, and provides a drug-use survey service. It conducts an annual conference; publishes a newsletter, a youth group handbook, and other publications; and sells and rents books, films, videos, and slide programs. membership is $20. The Hurt Building, 50 Hurt Plaza, Suite 210, Atlanta, GA 30303. Telephone (404) 577-4500; (800) 241-9746.

TARGET. Conducted by the National Federation of State High School Associations, an organization of interscholastic activities associations, TARGET offers workshops, training seminars, and an information bank on chemical use and prevention. It has a computerized referral service to substance abuse literature programs. National Federation of State High School Associations, 11724 Plaza Circle, P.O. Box 20626, Kansas City, MO 64195. Telephone (816) 464-5400.

Toughlove. This national self-help group for parents, children, and communities emphasizes cooperation, personal initiative, avoidance of blame, and action. It publishes a newsletter, brochures, and books and holds workshops. P.O. Box 1069, Doylestown, PA 18901. Telephone (800) 333-1069 or (215) 348-7090.

U.S. Clearinghouse. (A publication list is available on request, along with placement on a mailing list for new publications. Single copies are free.)

National Clearinghouse for Alcohol and Drug Information (NCADI) P.O. Box 2345 Rockville, MD 20852 (301) 468-2600 1-800-SAY NOTO

NCADI combines the clearinghouse activities previously administered by the National Institute on Alcoholism and Alcohol Abuse and the National Institute on Drug Abuse. The Department of Education contributes to the support of the clearinghouse, and provides anti-drug materials for free distribution.

Other Sources Of Materials On Legal Issues:

Council of School Attorneys, National School Boards Association (NSBA), provides a national forum on the practical legal problems faced by local public school districts and the attorneys who serve them. NSBA conducts programs and seminars and publishes monographs on a wide range of legal issues affecting public school districts. 1680 Duke Street, Alexandria, VA 22314, Telephone (703) 838-NSBA.

National Organization on Legal Problems of Education (NOLPE) is a non-profit, non-advocacy organization that disseminates information about current issues in school law. NOLPE publishes newsletters, serials books, and monographs on a variety of school law topics; hosts seminars; and serves as a clearinghouse for information on education law. 3601 SW 29th Street, Suite 223, Topeka, KS 66614. Telephone (913) 273-3550.

Part 7
How To Help Your Child
Become An A Student
A) Monitor Assignments:

Children are more likely to complete assignments successfully when parents monitor homework. How closely you need to monitor depends upon the age of your child, how independent she is, and how well she does in school. Whatever the age of your child, if assignments are not getting done satisfactorily, more supervision is needed. Here are some good ways to monitor assignments:

Ask About The School's Homework Policy:

At the start of the school year, ask the teacher:

1) What kinds of assignments will be given?
2) How long are children expected to take to complete them?
3) How does the teacher want you to be involved?

Teachers' expectations vary. Ask your child's teacher what you should do, Should you just check to make sure the assignment is done, or should you do something more? Some teachers want parents to go over the homework and point out errors, while others ask parents to simply check to make sure the assignment is completed. It's also a good idea to ask the teacher to call you if any problems with homework come up.

Be Available:

Elementary school students often like to have someone in the same room when working on assignments in case they have questions. If your child will be cared for by someone else, talk to that person about what you expect regarding homework. For an older child, if no one will be around, let him know you want him to begin work before you get home and call to remind him if necessary.

Look Over Completed Assignments:

It's usually a good idea to check to see that your elementary school child has finished her assignments. If your junior high student is having trouble finishing assignments, check his too. If you're not there when an assignment is finished, look it over when you get home. After the teacher returns completed homework, read the comments to see if your child has done the assignments satisfactorily.

Monitor Television Viewing:

American children on average spend far more time watching television than they do completing homework. In many homes, more homework gets done when television time is limited. Once you and your child have worked out a homework schedule, take time to discuss how much television and what programs she can watch. It's worth noting that television can be a learning tool. Look for programs that relate to what your child is studying in school, such as programs on history or science or dramatizations of children's literature. When you can, watch shows with your child, discuss them, and encourage follow-up activities such as reading or a trip to the museum.

B) How To Help — Provide Guidance:

The basic rule is, "Don't do the assignments yourself ." It's not your homework — it's your child's. "I've had kids hand in homework that's in their parents' handwriting," one Washington, DC-area eighth-grade teacher complains. Doing assignments for your child won't help him understand and use information. And it won't help him become confident in his own abilities.

It can be hard for parents to let children work through problems alone and learn from their mistakes. It's also hard to know where to draw the line between supporting and doing.

Different teachers have different ideas about the best way for parents to provide guidance. Here are a few suggestions with which most teachers agree:

Figure Out How Your Child Learns Bests:

If you understand something about style of learning that suits your child, it will be easier for you to help her.

If you've never thought about this style, observe your child. See if it works better alone or with someone else. If your child gets more done when working with someone else, he may want to complete some assignments with a brother or sister or a classmate. (Some homework, however, is meant to be done alone. Check with the teacher if you aren't sure.)

Other things to consider about learning style: Does your child learn things best when she can see them? If so, drawing a picture or a chart may help with some assignments.

For example, after reading her science book, she may not remember the difference between the tibia and the fibula. But by drawing a picture of the leg and labeling the bones, she can remember easily.

Does your child learn things best when he can hear them? He may need to listen to a story or have directions read to him. Too much written material or too many pictures or charts may confuse him.

Does your child understand some things best when she can handle or move them? An apple cut four or six or eight ways can help children learn fractions.

Help Your Child Get Organized:

It's a good idea to set a regular time for children to do homework. Put up a calendar in a place where you'll see it often and record assignments on it. If your child's not able to write yet, then do it for him until he can do it himself. Writing out assignments will get him used to the idea of keeping track of what's due and when. You may want to use an assignment book instead of a calendar.

A bag for books will make it easier to carry homework to and from school. Homework folders in which youngsters can tuck their assignments for safekeeping help many students stay organized.

Encourage Good Study Habits:

Teachers generally give students tips on how to study. But it takes time and practice to develop good habits. You can reinforce these habits at home. For example:

Help your child structure time in order to complete assignments. For example, if your eighth-grader has a biology report due in 3 weeks discuss all the steps she needs to take to complete it on time, including:

1)   Selecting a topic.
2)   Doing the research by looking up books and other materials on the topic and taking notes.
3)   Figuring out what questions to discuss.
4)   Drafting an outline.
5)   Writing a rough draft.
6)   Revising and completing the final draft.

Encourage your child to write down how much time she expects to spend on each step.

Help your child get started when he has to do research reports or other big assignments. Encourage him to use the library. If he isn't sure where to begin, have him ask the librarian for suggestions. If he's using a computer for on-line reference resources — whether the computer's at home, school, or the library — make sure he's getting whatever help he needs to use it properly. Many public libraries have homework centers where there are tutors or other kinds of one-on-one assistance. After your child has done the research, listen while he tells you the points he wants to make in the report.

Give practice tests. Help your third-grader prepare for a spelling test by saying the words while she writes them down. Then have her correct her own test.

Help your child avoid last-minute cramming. Review with your fifth-grader how to study for his social studies test well before it's to be given. You can have him work out a schedule of what he needs to do to, make up a practice test, and write down questions he's made up.

Talk with your child about how to take a test. Be sure she understands how important it is to read the instructions carefully and to keep track of the time and avoid spending too much time on any question.

Talk About The Assignments:

Ask your child questions. Talking can help him think through an assignment and break it down into small, workable parts. Here are some sample questions:

1) Do you understand what you're supposed to do? After your child has read the instructions, ask her to tell you in her own words what the assignment is about. (If your child can't read yet, the teacher may have sent home instructions that you can read to her.) Some schools have homework hotlines you can call for assignments in case your child misplaced a paper or was absent that day. If your child doesn't understand the instructions, read them with her and talk about the assignment. Are there words she doesn't understand? How can she find out what they mean? If neither you nor your child understands an assignment, call a classmate or contact the teacher.

2) What do you need to do to finish the assignment? Your child may want to talk through the steps with you (or make a written list of them, if he's able to.)

3) Do you need help in understanding how to do your work? See if your child needs to

learn more, for example, about subtracting fractions before she can do her assignment. Or find out if the teacher needs to explain to her again when to use capital and lowercase letters. If you understand the subject yourself, you may want to work through some examples with your child. But let her do the assignment herself.

4) Have you ever done any problems like the ones you're supposed to do right now? See if your child has already done similar problems that can guide him in completing these particular ones.

5) Do you have everything you need to do the assignment? Sometimes your child needs special supplies, such as colored pencils, metric rulers, maps, or reference books. As mentioned before, check with the teacher, school guidance counselor, or principal for possible sources of assistance if you can't provide needed supplies; and check with the local public library or school library for books and other information resources.

6) Does your answer make sense to you? Some times the response to a math problem doesn't seem logical, or the meaning of a paragraph your child has written is unclear. If that's the case, your child may need to check over the math problem or revise the paragraph.

If your child is still confused, ask:

1) How far have you gotten on the assignment? Let's try to figure it out if you're having a problem.

2) Do you need to review your notes (or reread a chapter in your textbook) before you do the assignment?

3) Are you still having problems? Maybe it would help to take a break or have a snack.

Give Praise:

People of all ages respond to praise. And children need encouragement from the people whose opinions they value most — their parents. "Good first draft of your book report!" or "You've done a great job" can go a lone way toward motivating your child to complete assignments.

Children also need to know when they haven't done their best work. Make criticism constructive. Instead of telling a third-grader, "You aren't going to hand in that mess, are you?" try, "The teacher will understand your ideas better if you use your best handwriting." Then give praise when a neat version is completed.

C) How To Help: Talk With Someone At School To Resolve Problems:

Homework hassles can often be avoided when parents and caregivers value, monitor, and guide their children's work on assignments. But, sometimes helping in these ways is not enough. Problems can still come up. If they do, the schools, teachers, parents, and students may need to work together to resolve them.

Share Concerns With the Teacher:

You may want to contact the teacher if:

1) Your child refuses to do her assignments, even though you've tried hard to get her to do them.

2) Instructions are unclear.

3) You can't seem to help your child get organized to finish the assignments.

4) You can't provide needed supplies or materials.

5) Neither you nor your child can understand the purpose of assignments.

6) The assignments are often too hard or too easy.

7) The homework is assigned in uneven amounts — for instance, no homework is given on Monday, Tuesday, or Wednesday, but on Thursday four of your child's teachers all make big assignments that are due the next day.

8) Your child has missed school and needs to make up assignments.

In some cases, the school guidance counselor may be helpful in resolving such problems.

Work With the School:

Communication between teachers and parents is very important in solving homework problems. Here are some important things to remember:

1) Talk with teachers early in the school year. Get acquainted before problems arise, and let teachers know that you want to be kept informed. Most elementary schools and many secondary schools invite parents to come to parent-teacher conferences or open houses. If your child's school doesn't provide such opportunities, call the teacher to set up a meeting.

2) Contact the teacher as soon as you suspect your child has a homework problem (as

well as when you think he's having any major problems with his schoolwork). Schools have a responsibility to keep parents informed, and you have a right to be upset if you don't find out until report card time that your child is having difficulties. On the other hand, sometimes parents figure out that a problem exists before the teacher does. By alerting the teacher, you can work together to solve a problem in its early stages.

3) Request a meeting with the teacher to discuss homework problems. Tell him briefly why you want to meet. You might say, "Rachel is having trouble with her math homework. I'm worried about why she can't finish the problems and what we might do to help her." Parents for whom English is a second language may need to make special arrangements, such as including another person who is bilingual.

Don't go straight to the principal without giving the teacher a chance to work out the problem with you and your child.

4) Approach the teacher with a cooperative spirit. Believe that the teacher wants to help you and your child, even if you disagree about something. It's hard to solve problems if teachers and parents view each other as enemies.

If you have a complaint, try not to put the teacher on the defensive. For example, avoid saying that you think the assignments are terrible even if you think so. You might say, "I'm glad Calvin is learning to add and subtract in the first grade, but he doesn't want to do his math work sheets. Can we find another way for him to learn the same material?" This might encourage the teacher to let Calvin (and the rest of his classmates) try another approach. Perhaps he can learn addition and subtractions by moving around buttons, sticks or shells.

5) Let the teacher know if your child is bored with assignments or finds them too hard or too easy. (Teachers also like to know when children are particularly excited about an assignment.) Of course, not all homework assignments can be expected to interest your child and be perfectly suited to her. Teachers just don't have time to tailor homework to the individual heeds of each student night after night. However, most teachers want to assign homework that children enjoy and can complete successfully, and they welcome feedback from parents.

Many times homework can be structured so that a wide range of children will find assignments interesting. For example:

A) Different approaches to the same topic or lesson can be offered to students.

B) Extra assignments can be given to students who want more challenge.

C) Specialized assignments can be given to students having trouble in a particular area.

6) While meeting with the teacher, explain what you think is going on. Also tell the teacher if you don't know what the problem is. Sometimes a child's version of what's going on isn't the same as the teacher's version. For example, your child may tell you that the teacher never explains assignments so he can understand them. But the teacher may tell you that your child isn't paying attention when assignments are given.

7) Work out a way to solve or lessen the problem. The strategy will depend on what the problem is, how severe it is, and the needs of your child. For instance:

A) Is the homework often too hard? Maybe your child has fallen behind and will need extra help from a teacher, parent, or tutor to catch up.

B) Does your child need to make up a lot of work because of absences? The first step might be working out a schedule with the teacher.

C) Has your child been diagnosed with a learning disability or is one suspected? If so, you'll need to make sure your child gets extra help, and the teacher may need to adjust some assignments.

D) Does your child need extra support, beyond what home and school can give? Ask the teacher, school guidance counselor, or principal if there are mentor programs in your community. Mentor programs pair a child with an adult volunteer who assists with the youngster's special needs, such as tutoring or career advice. There are many good mentor programs operating in schools, universities, community organizations, churches, and businesses.

8) Make sure communication is clear. Listen to the teacher and don't leave until you're sure you understand what's being said. Make sure, too, that the teacher understands what you have to say. If, after the meeting, you realize you don't understand something, call the teacher to double check.

It may help to summarize what you've agreed to do at the end of the meeting:

A) OK, so to keep track of Kim's assignments, I'll check her assignment book each night and write my initials by new assignments. Each day you'll check to make sure she's written down all new assignments in her book. That way we'll be certain that I know what her assignments are.

9) Follow up to make sure that the approach you agreed to is working. If the teacher told you, for example, that your child needs to spend more time practicing long division, check back in a month to talk about your child progress.

Homework can bring together children, parents, and teachers in a common effort to improve student learning. The younger your child is when you start to do the kinds of activities suggested in this section, the better.

Helping your child with homework is an opportunity to improve your child's chances of doing well in school and life. By helping your child with homework, you can help him learn important lessons about discipline and responsibility. You can open up lines of communication — between you and your child, and you and the school. You are in a unique position to help your child make connections between schoolwork and the "real world," and thereby bring meaning (and some fun) to your child's homework experience.

Whether you succeed in doing all of the activities suggested in this section is not what's most important. What's most important is that you are willing to take the time and make the effort to be involved in your child's education.

Parents and caregivers may also wish to learn about an innovative homework program called TIPS (Teachers Involve Parents in Schoolwork), which was developed at the federally funded Center on Families, Communities, Schools and Children's Learning at Johns Hopkins University. TIPS assignments are designed for elementary and middle grade students to do together with adult family members. Hands-on, interactive assignments that draw on real-life situations have been developed in language arts, math, science, and health. Information is available through the Center's Dissemination Office at Johns Hopkins University, 3505 North Charles St., Baltimore, MD 21218.

Part 8
Preparing Your Child For College

A Note To Parents:

American colleges and universities are the "jewels" of education worldwide The United States boasts a higher education system so excellent that "studying abroad" is an option — not a necessity — for students in America.

In order to put such educational excellence within reach of your children, you and your family can do a lot to help your students properly prepare — both academically and financially. First, your child will need to study hard at every level and take the courses in middle school and high school that lay the foundation for succeeding in college-level courses. Second, it is important for you and your child, at every level, to try to put money aside for college and to be well informed about sources of student financial aid for college.

This resource section is designed to help you plan ahead — with your child and your child's teachers and counselors — to ensure he or she is prepared academically for rigors of college and to save now and plan financially for the costs of a college education.

Because of the growing importance of a college education in today's rapidly changing economy, State governments, colleges, and the U.S. Department of Education (the largest supplier of student financial aid in America) are searching for better ways to provide financial aid to qualified students. For example, just in the past three years, proposals to improve the student college loan program, increases the maximum Pell grant, and create the national service AmeriCorps program have been made by President Clinton and passed by Congress. Still under consideration are proposals to allow a tax deduction for college tuition, increase the availability of work study opportunities to serve one million students annually, and help students and teachers have better access to technology in elementary and secondary classrooms.

To better prepare students to meet college requirements, many schools are committing themselves to strengthen their curricula, raise their standards in core subjects, and build local partnerships for better schools. A number of schools, entire communities, and states have begun addressing these challenges. President Clinton has also proposed other education initiatives that have been passed by bipartisan votes in Congress, to give parents, teachers, and principals additional opportunities to upgrade their local schools. The Goals 2000: Educate America Act is a source of funds to start up school improvement plans initiated and implemented by local schools and communities. Also, the improving America's Schools Act provides resources to schools needing extra help in teaching basic skills and, through its Eisenhower Professional Development Program, can help provide teachers with the training they need to teach to higher standards. The "venture funds" in the School-to-Work Opportunities Act can be used to link high schools, community colleges, and employers to give students new career pathways.

We recognize that the American family is the rock on which a solid education can and must be built. Thirty years of research clearly shows that family and community involvement in children's learning is key for getting children on the right path in life.

To promote better support for families in education, we have formed the Family Involvement Partnership for Learning, which consists of 250 parent, religious, business, and education organizations dedicated to creating "family-friendly" schools, businesses, and communities. Materials about the Partnership may be of interest to you and are available by calling 1-800-USA-LEARN.

Ultimately, the success of our students depends on the commitment of family members like you who are teaming up with other families, teachers, and your child's principal to improve your schools, and are taking the time to work directly with your children in order to help them learn to grow. Thank you for your interest in this book and for your commitment to the education of our Nation's youth. We hope that you find Preparing Your Child for College is a valuable resource that will make a difference in your child's life.

A) General Questions About College

Why Attend College?

A college degree can provide your child with many opportunities in life. A college education can mean:

Greater Knowledge:

A college education will increase your child's ability to understand developments in science and in society, to think abstractly and critically, to express thoughts clearly in speech and in writing, and to make wise decisions. These skills are useful both on and off the job.

Greater Potential:

A college education can help increase your child's understanding of the community, the Nation, and the world — as he or she explores interests, discovers new areas of knowledge, considers lifelong goals, and becomes a responsible citizen.

More Job Opportunities:

The world is changing rapidly. Many jobs rely on new technology and already require more brainpower than muscle power. In your child's working life, more and more jobs will require education beyond high school. With a college education, your child will have more jobs from which to choose.

More Money:

A person who attends college generally earns more than a person who does not. For example, in 1994, a person with a college degree from a four-year college earned approximately $12,500 more in that year than a person who did not go to college. Someone with a two-year associate's degree also tends to earn more than a high school graduate.

Some of these benefits of college may not be obvious to your child. Even though he or she has to make the final decision to attend college,

you can help in the decision-making process by learning about all aspects of college yourself and sharing what you learn with your child.

What Types Of Colleges Exist?

More than half of all recent high school graduates in the United States pursue some type of post-secondary education. In many other countries, a smaller percentage of students go on for more schooling after high school. However, in America, recent surveys show that most parents want their children to get some college education. There is a wide range of higher education options in the United States. For this reason, your child is likely to find a college well suited to his or her needs.

There are two basic types of post-secondary education institutions:

1) **Community, Technical, and Junior Colleges:** Many kinds of colleges offer programs that are less than four years in length. Most of these schools offer education and training programs that are two years in length or shorter. The programs often lead to a license, a certificate, an associate of arts (A.A.) degree, or an associate of applied science (A.A.S.) degree.

2) **Four-Year Colleges and Universities:** These schools usually offer a bachelor of arts (B.A.) or Bachelor of Science (B.S.) degree. Some also offer graduate and professional degrees.

Community, Technical, and Junior Colleges: Colleges with programs that are less than four years in length are often called community colleges, technical colleges, or junior colleges:

Community Colleges: These are public, two-year colleges. They mostly serve people from nearby communities and offer academic courses, technical courses, and continuing education courses. Public institutions are supported by state and local revenues.

Technical Colleges: These are generally colleges that have a special emphasis on education and training in technical fields. However, although some technical colleges offer academic courses and programs, not all technical colleges offer two-year programs that lead to an associate of arts or science degree. Technical colleges may be private or public. Junior colleges and community colleges that offer many technical courses are often called "technical colleges."

Junior Colleges: These are generally two-year colleges that are private institutions. Some junior colleges are residential and are attended by students who come from other parts of the country.

Some programs at two-year colleges lead to A.S. or A.A. degree in an academic discipline. These academic programs are often comparable to the first two years of a general academic program offered by a four-year college or university. In many cases, two-year degrees can be transferred to four-year schools and Credited toward a B.A. or B.S. degree.

Many junior and community colleges offer technical/occupational training, as well as academic courses. For example, many cardiovascular technicians, medical laboratory technicians, and computer technicians received their education and training at junior colleges, community colleges, and/or technical colleges.

Many junior, community and technical colleges offer technical programs in cooperation with local businesses, industry, public service agencies, or other organizations. Some of these programs are formally connected to education programs that students start in high school; they are often referred to as "tech-prep" or "school-to-career" programs.

Two-year colleges such as community colleges often operate under an "open admissions" policy that can vary from school to school. At some institutions, "open admissions" means that anyone who has a high school diploma or GED certificate can enroll. At other schools, anyone over 18 years of age can enroll or, in some cases, anyone deemed able to benefit from the programs at the schools can enroll.

Application requirements at colleges with two-year programs and shorter programs may include a high school transcript — a list of all the courses your child took and grades earned in four years of high school — and college entrance examination scores as well. Some schools have programs that allow "open admissions," while other programs in the same school — particularly in scientific or technical subjects — may have further admission requirements. Since requirements vary widely, it is important to check into schools and programs individually.

Four-Year Colleges and Universities:

Students who wish to pursue a general academic program usually choose a four-year college or university. Such a program lays the foundation for more advanced studies and professional work. Four-year colleges and universities offer bachelor's degrees (the B.A. and B.S.) in most areas in the arts and sciences, such as English literature, foreign languages, history, economics, political science, biology, zoology, chemistry, and in many other fields.

Here are the main differences between four-year colleges and universities:

Four-year Colleges: These are post-secondary schools that provide four-year educational programs in the arts and sciences. These colleges confer bachelor's degrees.

Universities: These are post-secondary schools that include a college of arts and/or sciences, one or more programs of graduate studies, and one or more professional schools. Universities confer bachelor's degrees and graduate and professional degrees.

When a student earns a bachelor's degree it means that he or she has passed examinations in a broad range of courses and has studied one or two subject areas in greater depth. (These one or two subject areas are called a student's "major" area(s) of study or area(s) of "concentration.") A bachelor's degree is usually required before a student can begin studying for a graduate degree. A graduate degree is usually earned through two or more years of advanced studies beyond four years of college. This might be a master's or a doctoral degree in a particular field or a specialized degree required in certain professions such as law, social work, architecture, or medicine.

What Kinds Of Jobs Are Available To College Graduates?

Certificates and degrees earned by graduates of two-and four-year colleges or universities usually lead to different kinds of professional opportunities. Many professions require graduate degrees beyond the traditional four-year degree, such as a medical degree or a law degree. For example:

1) A course study in bookkeeping at a community college generally prepares a student for a job as a bookkeeper.

2) A four-year degree in economics may prepare a student for any one of several jobs in a bank or a business.

3) A four-year degree in English may serve as background for getting teacher certification in the subject or for being an editor with a magazine.

In the following chart there is a partial listing of different occupations and the educational background generally required or recommended for each. Some people who go on to acquire jobs in the four-year-college column obtain a graduate degree or some graduate education, but many of these jobs can be filled by people who do not have more than a four-year college education. For more information on the educational requirements of specific jobs, contact a guidance counselor or check the Occupational Outlook Handbook in your library (See the following section for more information and other publications that discuss jobs.)

CHART 1
Example of Jobs Requiring College Preparation
Two-Year College
(Associate's Degree)

Surveyor	Automotive Mechanic
Registered Nurse	Administrative Assistant
Dental Hygienist	Cardiovascular Technician
Medical Laboratory	Medical Record Technician
Computer Technician	Surgical Technologist
Commercial Artist	Water and Wastewater Treatment Plant Operator
Hotel/Restaurant	Heating, Air-Conditioning, and Refrigeration Technician
Funeral Director	Engineering Technician
Drafter	

CHART 1 (cont.)
Four-Year College
(Bachelor's Degree)

Teacher	Writer
Accountant	Editor
FBI Agent	Graphic Designer
Engineer	Social Worker
Journalist	Recreational Therapist
Diplomat	Public Relations Specialist
Insurance Agent	Visual Artist
Pharmacist	Research Assistant
Computer System Analyst	Investment Banker
Dietitian	Medical Illustrator

More Than Four Years of College
(Various Graduate Degrees Required)

Lawyer	Public Policy Analyst
Architect	Geologist
Doctor	Paleontologist
Scientist	Zoologist
University Professor	Rabbi
Economist	Priest
Psychologist	Chiropractor
Sociologist	Biologist
Dentist	Management Consultant
Veterinarian	

B) Preparing For College

What Can My Child Do To Prepare Academically For College?

Take Courses Recommended for College-Bound Students:

To prepare for college, there is no substitute for your child getting a solid and broad academic education. This means your child should take challenging courses in academic subjects and maintain good grades in high school. Your child's transcript will be an important part of his or her college application.

A college education builds on the knowledge and skills acquired in earlier years. It is best for your child to start planning a high school course schedule early, in the seventh or eighth grade. Students who don't plan ahead may have difficulty completing all the required or recommended courses that will help them qualify for college.

Most selective colleges (those with the highest admissions requirements) prefer to admit students who have taken courses in certain subject areas. For example, many colleges prefer that high school students take at least geometry and trigonometry, rather than only general math and algebra. Basic computer skills are now essential, and some colleges prefer three or four years of a foreign language. Your child's guidance counselor can help your child determine the high school courses required or preferred by different types of colleges. If your child is interested in specific colleges, he or she can contact those schools and ask about their admissions requirements.

Many high schools offer Advanced Placement (AP) courses and exams. AP courses are college-level courses in approximately 16 different subjects; they help students prepare for college-level work while they are still in high school Students who take AP courses are often more prepared for the academic challenges presented in college. In addition, a student who takes an AP course and who scores a grade of 3 or higher on an AP exam can often receive advance placement in college and/or credit for a college course. Talk to one of your child's teachers, your child's guidance counselor, or the principal of your child's school to find out if AP courses are offered at your child's high school.

Chart 2 lists the high school courses that many higher education associations and guidance counselors recommend for a college-bound student. These courses are especially recommended for students who want to attend a four-year college. Even if your child is interested in attending a junior college, community college, or technical college, he or she should take most of these courses since they provide the preparation necessary for all kinds of post-secondary education (In addition, many students who attend two-year colleges go on to earn a B.A. or B.S. degree at a four year college or university.)

Traditional English courses such as American and English literature will help students improve their writing skills, reading comprehension, and vocabulary. History and geography will help your child better understand our society as well as societies around the world.

Mathematical and scientific concepts and skills learned in math classes are used in many disciplines outside of these courses. A recent study showed that students who take algebra and geometry in high school are much more likely to go on to college than students who do not. Research also indicates that students who take courses in the arts disciplines and who participate in the arts and visual arts often do better in school and on standardized tests. The arts help students to learn; they often give students a richer understanding of history, science, literature, and math.

Thirty states require students to take some art courses(s) (visual or performing) before graduating from high school; six state university systems require students to take at least one unit of art (visual or performing) at the high school level before gaining admission to the university. Many college admissions staff view participation in the arts as a valuable experience that broadens students' understanding and appreciation of the world around them.

Things You And Your Child Can Do To Prepare For A Technical Program At A Community, Junior, Or Technical College:

If your child is interested in pursuing a technical program in a community, junior, or technical college, he or she may want to supplement or substitute some of the courses listed in the chart with some vocational or technical courses in his or her field of interest. Look especially for more advanced technology courses in the junior and senior years of high school.

Talking to an administrator or professor from a community, junior, or technical college is a good way to find out about the best high school courses to take in order to prepare for a specific technical program offered at that college. The dean of a particular technical program will also be able to tell you about the entry requirements for the program.

You may want to ask educators at a local college (or staff at your child's school) about educational programs that have formal connections between the high school and the local college. There are many career-focused programs that are offered by a network of high schools, local colleges, and sometimes, local employers. Many of these programs are known as "tech-prep," "2+2," or "school-to-career" programs. The high school course work in these programs is formally linked to the course work offered at the local colleges. In this way, the high school material better prepares students for the college-level work. It also starts the student on a clear path toward a college degree.

"Tech-prep" and "2+2" programs often refer to educational programs offered by networks of school districts and colleges. Such programs offer students career pathways that link their high school classes to advanced technical education in colleges or apprenticeship programs. These programs are often called "2+2" programs because they span the last two years of high school and the first two years of college. Thus, they are four-year programs.

These programs emphasize applied learning—the teaching of academic material through hands-on experience. In addition, students in "tech-prep" and "2+2" programs receive extensive academic and career guidance from counselors and teachers.

"School-to-career" or "school-to-work" are the terms that often refer to career-focused programs that have many of the same elements as "tech-prep" and "2+2" programs. In addition, "school-to-career" programs also provide students with the opportunity to learn in a real work setting. Students have the opportunity to spend time at a local work site where they can apply their skills and acquire new ones. You can learn more about career-focused education programs by talking to educators in your community.

Chart 2
High School Courses Recommended For College

Although academic requirements differ across colleges the admissions requirements listed below are typical of four-year colleges. The specific classes listed here are examples of the types of courses students can take.

English — 4 years
Types of classes:

Composition	English literature
American literature	World literature

Mathematics — 3 to 4 years
Types of classes:

Algebra I	Trigonometry
Algebra 2	Pre-calculus
Geometry	Calculus

Laboratory Science — 2 to 3 years
Types of classes:

Biology	Chemistry
Earth science	Physics

Foreign Language — 2 to 3 years
Types of classes:

French	Latin
German	Russian
Spanish	Japanese

History & Geography — 2 to 3 years
Types of classes:

Geography	World history
U.S. history	World cultures
U.S. government	Civics

Chart 2 (cont.)
Visual & Performing Arts — 1 year
Types of classes:

Art   Drama
Dance   Music

Appropriate Electives—1 to 3 years
Types of classes:

Economics   Computer science
Psychology   Communications
Statistics

Make Sure That All Courses Meet High Standards:

It is not only important for your child to enroll in the courses recommended for college in-bound students; it is also essential that the material taught in those courses reflect high academic standards and high expectations for what students should know and be able to do. Research indicates that high expectations and high standards improve achievement and positively influence student learning.

Efforts are under way in states and communities across the country to answer the question: "What is it that our children ought to know and be able to do... to participate fully in today's and tomorrow's economy?" Many states and local communities have been developing or revising their standards (sometimes called "curriculum frameworks") in core subject areas such as math, science, English, history, geography, foreign language, civics, and the arts. These standards help provide parents with answers to questions such as:

"Is my child learning?"

"What is it that my child should know by the end of each grade?"

Many school districts are not waiting for their states to complete standards. In many local communities, groups of citizens — parents, teachers, administrators, business leaders, clergy, representatives from colleges, curriculum experts, and other community

nity members —are working together to develop or revise standards. In creating their own standards, many states and local communities are drawing on model voluntary standards developed by national professional associations.

In order to make sure that the curriculum in your child's school meets high academic standards, call your child's school to find out if state or local standards are being developed. Ask how you can get involved in the standard-setting process. Join with other parents, teachers, and your child's principal and compare your school's standards against the best schools and the best state standards. You can also learn about the voluntary standards developed by national professional associations by contacting the professional organizations listed in the back of this section.

Take The Standardized Tests That Many Colleges Require:

Many of the courses recommended for college-bound students (such as geometry and rigorous English courses) are also essential preparation for the college entrance examinations — the SAT 1 (Scholastic Assessment Test) or the ACT (Assessment Test) or the ACT Assessment. The SAT 1 measures verbal and mathematical reasoning abilities. The ACT Assessment measures English, mathematics, reading, and science reasoning abilities. Students applying to colleges in the East and West usually take the SAT 1 exam. Students applying to schools in the South and Midwest often take the ACT. (However, students should check the admission requirements at each school to which they are applying.)

Usually, the tests are offered in the junior and senior years of high school and can be taken more than once if a student wishes to try to improve his or her score. Students can get books at libraries or bookstores to help them to prepare for all of the tests. Some of these books are listed at the back of this section. In addition, some private organizations and companies offer courses that help students prepare for these exams.

Many schools offer the Preliminary Scholastic Assessment Test/National Merit Scholarship Qualifying Test (PSAT/NMSQT) to their students. This practice test helps students prepare for the Scholastic Assessment Test (SAT 1). The PSAT is usually administered to tenth or eleventh grade students. A student who does very well on this test and who meets many other academic performance criteria may qualify for the National Merit Scholarship Program. You and your child can find out more about the PSAT/NMSQT and the National Merit Scholarship Program by talking to your child's guidance counselor or by calling or writing to the number or address provided in the back of this section.

Some colleges also require that an applicant take one or more SAT 2 Subject Tests in major areas of study. It is a good idea for a student to consult a guidance counselor about this early in high school; often the best time to take an SAT 2 Test is right after the student has taken a course in that subject. For example, many students take the biology SAT 2 Test right after they have completed a course in biology. This could mean that your child would take his or her first SAT 2 Test as a freshman or sophomore in high school.

At the end of this section you will find the address and phone number where you can write or call for more information about the SAT 1 and the SAT 2 Tests. You will also find the address and phone number for the organization that administers the ACT.

Knowing what will be required for college is important; by taking the right courses and examinations from the beginning of high school, your child may avoid admission problems later on. In addition, students who do not prepare well enough academically in high school, if admitted to college, may be required to take remedial courses. Most colleges do not offer credit for these courses, and students may have to pay for these extra courses and spend extra time in college to earn their degrees. Chart 3 lists some questions that you or your child may want to ask your child's guidance counselor.

CHART 3
Questions To Ask Guidance Counselors

1) What basic academic courses do they recommend for students who want to go to college?
2) How many years of each academic subject does the high school require for graduation?
3) What elective courses do they recommend for college-bound students?
4) How does a student go about completing recommended courses before graduating from high school?
5) Can students who are considering college get special help or tutoring?
6) What activities can students do at home and-over the summers to strengthen their preparation for college?
7) How much homework is expected of students preparing for college?
8) What kinds of high school grades do different colleges require?

What Can My Child Do Outside The Classroom To Prepare For College?

Interpersonal and leadership skills, interests and goals are all important for college preparation. Independent reading and study, extracurricular activities, and work experience will all help your child develop his or her skills, interests, and goals.

Independent Reading And Study:

Independent reading and study will help your child to prepare academically for college. This is a good way to develop interests, expand knowledge, and improve the vocabulary and reading comprehension skills needed for college and the SAT 1 or ACT. Encourage your child to read all kinds of books for fun — fiction and nonfiction. The school library and the local public library are good sources of books, magazines, and newspapers.

Creating A Good Place To Study:

Your child needs a quiet and comfortable place to study. Here are a few things that you can do:

1) Help him or her find a quiet place with some privacy.

2) Set up a desk or large table with good light and place reference books — such as a

dictionary on the desk or-nearby.

3)   Make sure your child studies there on a regular basis.

Extracurricular Activities:

Many school, community, and religious organizations enable high school students to explore their interest and talents by providing activities outside the classroom. Colleges are often interested in a student's extracurricular activities such as school clubs, the student newspaper, athletics, musical activities, arts, drama, and volunteer work, especially if a student has excelled in one or more of these areas.

Work Experience And Community Service:

Work experience — paid or volunteer — can teach students discipline, responsibility, reliability, teamwork, and other skills. Some students participate in community service activities such as tutoring elementary school children or volunteering in a local hospital. Such activities make valuable contributions to society and also help students to identify their career interests and goals, gain workplace skills, and apply classroom learning to real-world problem solving. Many colleges view community service as a valuable experience that enhances a student's college application.

Some schools offer academic credit for volunteer work through "service-learning." This is a teaching method that integrates hands-on learning (through service to the community) into the school curriculum. To find out if your child's school offers "service-learning," talk to your child's teacher, guidance counselor, or school principal. For information on how to start a "service-learning" program, contact the Learn and Serve America Clearinghouse at 1-800-808-SERVE.

A summer job is also a good way to gain experience and earn money for college as well. If your child works during the school year, he or she should not work so many hours that the job interferes with schoolwork.

C) Choosing A College

How Can My Child Go About Choosing A College?

Colleges are located in big cities, suburbs, and small towns throughout the country. Some enroll tens of thousands of students; others enroll only a few hundred. Some are public; others are private. Some private institutions are affiliated with religious institutions; others are not. Some schools enroll only women, others only men.

The type of institution best suited to your child depends on his or her individual needs and talents. Your child can begin focusing on the choice of a college by considering the following questions:

1) Why do I want to go to college?

2) What do I hope to achieve in college?

3) Do I have some idea of what I want to study or for which job I want to prepare?

4) Do I want to live at home or go away to school?

5) Do I prefer an urban or suburban environment?

6) Would I be happier in a small college or at a large university?

In order to choose a college, you and your child should ask the following questions about the nature and quality of the schools in which your child has an interest. (Ask these questions when you meet staff in the admissions office of the colleges. You may also find answers to these questions in the colleges' catalogs or in reference books on colleges.)

The Nature Of The Education Offered:

◆ What is the philosophy of the particular college, and what kinds of educational programs does this college offer?

Ask about the college's specialties, which types of classes the school offers, and in which fields students can earn a degree or certificate. How many students study in each area, and what do they do when they graduate?

◆ How long does it take to earn a certificate or degree at this college?

Students should know how much time it takes to complete a program before they enroll in it. Programs can last anywhere from a few months to several years. Also ask whether the time involved reflects full-time or part-time attendance.

◆ What do students do when they graduate from this school? Do they get jobs in the areas for which they were trained? Do they pursue further education?

Job placement rates are particularly important for vocational programs. If a very low percentage of students are employed in their area of training year after completing the program, there may be a problem. It can also be useful to ask about beginning salaries of program graduates and the institution's career advising and placement services for its students.

Students who enroll in two-year colleges with plans to transfer to four-year colleges should inquire about the possibility of doing so and about the number of graduates who transfer each year. Students applying to four-year colleges may want to know how many graduates go on to graduate or profession education.

The Quality Of The College:

◆ How many students who start at this school earn a certificate or degree? How many drop out?

A high dropout rate may suggest that students are dissatisfied with the education an institution provides. Be particularly careful about having your child enroll in a school that graduates a very low percentage of its students. Also ask about tuition refunds policies for students who drop out in the first weeks of an educational program.

◆ What is the loan default rate at this college? Do students repay their student loans?

The default rate is the percentage of students who took out student loans to help pay their expenses but did not repay them properly. A high default rate may suggest that students who borrowed never completed their educational program, or that they were unable to find jobs and repay the loans when they graduated. Colleges with consistently high default rates may be barred from student loan programs, and students attending these institutions may thus be ineligible for federal loans.

◆ Have other students who have gone to this college liked it? What has their experience been?

Colleges should be able to refer you to current students or recent graduates of their programs. These individuals can give you their opinion about classes, facilities, the faculty (teachers), and the skills they have learned.

◆ What kinds of facilities does this college have? Are they adequate for my child's needs?

You and your child should consider the condition of classrooms, libraries, and dormitories when choosing a college. The types of facilities appropriate for a college depend on the type of education provided. For example, a college offering classes in the sciences should have modern laboratories, and an institution that offers computer education classes should have adequate computer facilities.

Admissions Requirements And Financial Aid:

◆ What admissions requirements does this college have?

Each institution can require students to take certain high school classes and submit certain items with their applications. Make sure you know what is required by the schools that interest your child.

◆ Is this college accredited by an agency recognized by the Secretary of Education and eligible to participate in Federal student aid programs?

Federal financial aid is available only to students attending eligible institutions. Students attending other institutions cannot receive federal financial aid. If you are interested in having your child apply for federal financial aid, be wary of unaccredited institutions and those with high default rates. You can call the Federal Student Financial Aid Information Center toll-free to find out if a particular college is an eligible institution. The number is 1-800-4FED-AID.

D) Financing A College Education
How Much Does A College Education Cost?

Many people overestimate the cost of college or believe that all schools are expensive. For example, a recent Gallup survey indicated that 13-to 21-year-olds overestimated the average cost of public two-and four-year colleges by more than three times the actual figure. The same group estimated that the costs of private four-year colleges were one-third higher than they actually were.

Although some colleges are expensive, costs vary from institution to institution. In addition, the availability of financial aid — money available from various sources to help students pay for college — can make even an expensive college affordable for a qualified student.

College Costs:

The basic costs of college are tuition, fees, and other expenses:

1) Tuition

Tuition is the amount of money that colleges charge for instruction and for the use of some facilities, such as libraries. Tuition can range from a few hundred dollars per year to more than $20,000. The least costly option for post-secondary education is typically a local community college where the average tuition and fees are generally under $1,500 per year. There are also many four-year colleges and universities that are relatively inexpensive. For example, a little less than half of the students who attend four-year colleges go to institutions that charge less than $3,000 in tuition and fees. This occurs because about 68 percent of the students who attend four-year colleges attend public institutions whose tuitions are much lower than those of private institutions.

2) Fees

Fees are charges (usually small) that cover costs generally not associated with the student's course load, such as costs of some athletic activities student activities, clubs, and special events.

3) Other Expenses

Besides tuition and fees, students at most colleges and universities pay for room, board, books, supplies, transportation, and other miscellaneous costs. "Room and board" refers to the cost of housing and food.

Tuition At Public and Private Colleges:

It is important to know the difference between public and private institutions. A school's private or public status has a lot to do with its tuition.

1) Public Institutions

Over three-quarters of all students in two-and four-year colleges attend state or other public colleges. Since these schools receive a large proportion of their budgets from state or local government, they can charge students who live in that state (in-state students) relatively low tuition. Students from other states (out-of-state students) usually pay higher tuition.

In 1995-96, in-state students attending public four-year colleges faced an average tuition and fees of $2,860 per year. In-state students at public two-year colleges faced an average tuition and fees of $1,387 per year in 1995-96. Tuition and fees for out-of-state or out-of-district students at public institutions averaged $2,775 and $4,508 at two-year and four-year colleges, respectively.

If the cost of room, board, books, supplies, transportation, and other personal expenses are added to tuition and fees, the average total cost of attending a public four-year college was $9,285 in 1995-96. Since many students who attend two-year public schools live at home, the average total cost of attending a two-year public college in 1995-96 was $5,752. This includes the cost of tuition, fees, books, supplies, transportation and other personal expenses for a commuter student.

2) Private Institutions

Private (sometimes called "independent") institutions charge the same tuition for both in-state and out-of-state students. Private college tuitions tend to be higher than those of public colleges because private schools receive less financial support from states and local governments

Most private colleges are "non-profit." Other private post-secondary schools — mostly vocational and trade schools — are "proprietary." Such institutions are legally permitted to make a profit. Students at private colleges in 1995-96 faced an average tuition and fees of $12,432 per year at four-year colleges and $6,350 per year at two-year non-profit colleges.

If the cost of room, board, books, supplies, transportation, and other personal expenses are added to tuition and fees, the average total cost of attending a private four-year college was $19,762 in 1995-96. If these same kinds of cost are added to the tuition and fees of a two-year private college, the average total cost of attending such a school was $12,710 in 1995-96.

Future College Costs:

By the time your child is ready to attend college, the tuition, fees, and cost of room, board, and other expenses will be larger than the amounts discussed in this section. Because there are many factors that affect the costs of a college education, it is impossible to know exactly how much colleges will charge when your child is ready to enroll. Be cautious when people tell you a particular amount; no one can be sure how much cost will change over time. In addition, as college cost increase, the amount of money you earn, and thus the amount you will have available to pay for college, will also rise.

How Can I Afford To Send My Child To College?

Saving money in advance and obtaining financial aid are common ways for parents to make their child's education affordable. Other ways of making college affordable, such as attending college part time, will be discussed later in this section.

Saving Money:

Saving money is the primary way to prepare for the cost of college. Setting aside a certain amount every month or each payday will help build up a fund for college. If you and your child begin saving early, the amount you have to set aside each month will be smaller.

In order to set up a savings schedule, you'll need to think about where your child might attend college, how much that type of college might cost, and how much you can afford to save. Keep in mind that colleges of the same type have a range of costs and your child may be able to attend one that is less expensive. You can also pay part of the costs from your earnings while your child is attending school. In addition, your child may also be able to meet some of the costs of college by working during the school year or during the summer. Finally, some federal, state, or other student financial aid may be available, including loans to you and to your child.

You will also want to think about what kind of savings instrument to use or what kind of investment to make. By putting your money in some kind of savings instrument or investment, you can set aside small amounts of money regularly and the money will earn interest or dividends. Interest refers to the amount that your money earns when it is kept in a savings instrument. Dividends are payments of part of a company's earnings to people who hold stock in the company.

A savings instrument has an "interest rate" associated with it; this refers to the rate at which the money in the instrument increases over a certain period of time. Principal refers to the face value or the amount of money you place in the savings instrument on which the interest is earned.

Chart 4 shows how much you would need to save each month in order to have $10,000 available when your child begins college. As the chart demonstrates, the amount varies depending on the interest rate you obtain and the number of years that you save. The higher the interest rate and the earlier you begin to save, the less you need to set aside each month.

For example, if you start saving when your child is born, you will have 18 years to save. As shown on the chart, each month you will only have to deposit $32 in an account earning 4 percent interest in order to save $10,099 by the time your child is 18. However, if you use the same savings instrument but do not start to save until your child is 16, you will have to save $401 each month. In addition, if you use the instrument with the higher interest rate — 8 percent — you will only have to put away $21 each month starting when your child is born.

Remember, by starting to save early and by using instruments with higher interest rates, you can put aside smaller amounts. If you wait until later to start saving, you may not be able to afford to put away the larger amounts of money needed to meet your savings goals.

CHART 4

Amount You Would Need To Save To Have $10,000 Available When Your Child Begins College

Amount Available When Child Begins College
(Assuming a 4 percent interest rate.)

If you start saving when your child is	Number of years of saving	Monthly savings	Interest principal	Total earned	Total savings
Newborn	18	$ 32	$6,912	$3,187	$10,099
Age 4	14	45	7,560	2,552	10,112
Age 8	10	68	8,160	1,853	10,013
Age 12	6	124	8,928	1,144	10,072
Age 16	2	401	9,624	378	10,002

(Assuming an 8 percent interest rate.)

If you start saving when your child is	Number of years of saving	Monthly savings	Interest principal	Total earned	Total savings
Newborn	18	$ 21	$4,536	$5,546	$10,082
Age 4	14	33	5,544	4,621	10,165
Age 8	10	55	6,660	3,462	10,062
Age 12	6	109	7,848	2,183	10,031
Age 16	2	386	9,264	746	10,010

When deciding which type of savings instrument or investment is right for you and your family, you should consider four features:

◆ **Risk:**

The danger that the money you set aside could be worth less in the future.

◆ **Return:**

The amount of money you earn on the savings instrument or investment through interest or dividends.

◆ **Liquidity:**

How quickly you can gain access to the money in the instrument or investment.

◆ **Time Frame:**

The number of years you will need to save or invest.

When you select one or more savings instruments or investments, you should balance these factors by minimizing the risk while maximizing the return on your money. You will also want to be sure that you will be able to access the money at the time you need to pay for your child's education.

If you start early enough, you may feel confident about making some long-term investments. Some investments are riskier than others but can help you earn more money over time. You can get more information on these and other savings instruments at local banks and at your neighborhood library.

Don't forget that you won't necessarily have to save for the entire cost of college. The following section tells about student financial aid for which you and your child might qualify and other ways to keep college cost down.

Financial Aid:

Financial aid can help many families meet college costs. Every year millions of students apply for and receive financial aid. In fact, almost one-half of all students who go on for more education after high school receive financial aid of some kind. In school year 1994 -95, post-secondary students received about $47 billion in financial aid.

There are three main types of financial assistance available to qualified students at the college level:

◆ **Grants and Scholarships**

◆ **Loans**

◆ **Work-Study.**

Grants and Scholarships:

Grants and scholarships provide aid that does not have to be repaid. However, some require that recipients maintain certain grade levels or take certain courses.

Loans:

Loans are another type of financial aid and are available to both students and parents. Like a car loan or a mortgage for a house, an education loan must eventually be repaid. Often, payments do not begin until the student finishes school, and the interest rate on education loans is commonly lower than for other types of loans. For students with no established credit record, it is usually easier to get student loans than other kinds of loans.

There are many different kinds of education loans. Before taking out any loan, be sure to ask the following kinds of questions:

◆ **What are the exact provisions of the loan?**

◆ **What is the interest rate?**

◆ **Exactly how much has to be paid in interest?**

◆ **What will the monthly payments be?**

◆ **When will the monthly payments begin?**

◆ **How long will the monthly payments last?**

◆ **What happens if you miss one of the monthly payments?**

◆ **Is there a grace period for paying back the loan?**

In all cases, a loan taken to pay for a college education must be repaid, whether or not a student finishes school or gets a job after graduation. Failure to repay a student loan can ruin a person's credit rating and make finances much more difficult in the future. This is important reason to consider a college's graduation and job placement rates when you help your child choose a school.

Work-Study Programs:

Many students work during the summer and/or part time during the school year to help pay for college. Although many obtain jobs on their own, many colleges also offer work-study programs to their students. A work-study job is often part of a student's financial aid package. The jobs are usually on campus and the money earned is used to pay for tuition or other college charge.

The types of financial aid discussed above can be merit-based, need-based, or a combination of merit-based and need-based.

Merit-Based Financial Aid:

Merit-based assistance, usually in the form of scholarships or grants, is given to students who meet requirements not related to financial needs. For example, a merit scholarship may be given to a student who has done well in high school or one who display artistic or athletic talent. Most merit-based aid is awarded on the basis of academic performance or potential.

Need-Based Financial Aid:

Need-based means that the amount of aid a student can receive depends on the cost of the college and on his or her family's ability to pay these costs. Most financial aid is need-based and is available to qualified students.

What Are The Most Common Sources Of Financial Aid?

Student financial aid is available from a number of sources, including the federal government, state governments, colleges and universities, and other organizations. Students can receive aid from more than one source.

Federal Financial Assistance:

The federal government supplies the largest amount of all student aid, about 75 percent or $35 billion annually. The largest and most popular Federal student aid programs are:

u   **Federal Pell Grant:**

These are need-based grants that were given to just under 4 million students for school year 1994-95. In school year 1995-96, the maximum Pell Grant was $2,340.

u   **Federal Stafford Loans:**

There are two types of Stafford Loans — subsidized and unsubsidized. Subsidized loans are need-based and unsubsidized loans are non-need-based. In 1994-95, approximately 6 million students received Stafford Loans.

With a subsidized loan, the federal government pays the interest on the loan while the student is in school and for six months after graduation while the student is seeking employment. The student than starts paying back the loan with interest after the six-month "grace period."

With an unsubsidized loan, the interest accrues while the student is in school. After graduation, the student must pay back the loan and the interest on the loan, including the interest that accrued while the student was in school.

For both types of loans, the loan limits are $2,625 for the first year, $3,500 for the second year, and $5,500 for the third or more years. An undergraduate cannot borrow more than a total of $23,000.

u   Federal PLUS Loans:

Federal PLUS Loans allow parents to borrow money for their children's college education. The yearly limit is the cost of education minus any estimated financial aid for which the student is eligible.

More Information About Federal Stafford And Plus Loans:

In the past, students and parents could only receive Federal loans (including Stafford and Plus Loans) through banks or other lenders under the Federal Family Education Loan (FFEL) Program. Beginning July 1, 1994, the federal government began to phase in a new program called the William D. Ford Federal Direct Loan Program. Under this program some colleges and universities provide Federal Stafford Loans (both subsidized and unsubsidized) and Federal PLUS Loans directly to students and parents with funds provided by the Federal Government through the U.S. Department of Education.

The intent of the Direct Loan Program is to provide a simpler and faster way to obtain loans. Direct Loans are currently being offered at approximately 1,350 schools. Students who attend schools that are not participating in the Direct Loan program will continue to obtain their loans from banks or other lenders under the FFEL Program.

The terms of the loans are basically the same under the FFEL and Direct Loan Programs. The difference is that Direct Loan borrowers will repay their loans to the U.S. Department of Education rather than to a bank or other lender.

A key goal of the Direct Loan Program is to allow students to pick a repayment plan that best fits their financial circumstances. Under Direct Loans, a borrower may choose from among four different repayment plans, including the Income Contingent Repayment Plan where the monthly payment is based on the borrower's annual income and the amount borrowed. Increasingly, lenders under the FFEL Program are also providing a variety of repayment options.

Federal Campus-Based Programs:

The Federal Government provides money to colleges to give to needy through three

Federal Campus-Based Programs. These three programs include

1) A grant program (Federal Supplemental Educational Opportunity Grants, or SEOGs,

2) A loan program (Federal Perkins Loans), and

3) The Federal Work Study Program.

More Information on Federal Aid:

Students can get aid from more than one federal program. For the most up-to-date information about student aid supplied by the Federal Government, call the Federal Student Financial Aid Information Center toll-free at the U.S. Department of Education at 1-800-4FED-AID. You can also obtain a guide to federal financial aid for students called The Student Guide, which provides an extensive and annually updated discussion of all federal student aid programs. You can obtain the guide by writing to the following address:

Federal Student Aid Information Center
P.O. Box 84
Washington, DC 20044
Call: (800) 4FED-AID

State Financial Assistance:

States generally give portions of state budgets to public colleges and universities. This support lowers tuition for all students attending these schools. Some states also offer financial assistance directly to individual students, which can be need-based or merit-based. To find out about state aid where you live, call or write your state's higher education agency. The phone numbers and addresses of all of these agencies are listed in the following section.

College/University Assistance:

Colleges themselves provide aid to many of their students. Most of this "institutional aid" is in the form of scholarships or grants. Some is need-based and some is merit-based.

When your child wants financial aid information about specific schools, he or she should contact the financial aid offices of these schools and request information.

Other Types of Assistance:

Other organizations, such as corporations, labor unions, professional associations, religious organizations and credit unions, sometimes award financial aid. You can find out about the availability of such scholarships by contacting someone from the specific organization or by directly contacting its main headquarters.

In addition, some organizations, particularly foundations, offer scholarships to minorities, women, and disabled students. To learn more about such scholarships, go to the nearest public library with a good reference section and look for directories that list such scholarships. (The names of a few books that list scholarships appear in the following section.) College admissions offices and high school guidance counselors should also be able to provide more information about scholarships.

Help in Getting More Information:

The guidance counselors at your child's high school should be able to provide information on when and how to apply for federal, state, and other types of aid. If they cannot give you this information, try a local college. Even if your child doesn't plan to attend that particular institution, financial aid officers there should have information on financial aid. Many colleges can also tell you about state aid and their own institutional aid.

Is My Child Eligible For Financial Ail? If So, How Much?

To qualify for federal aid, you or your child must submit a financial aid application. Applications for financial aid request information about your family's income, savings, and assets, as well as information on the number of children in the family who are in college. You can get a copy of the federal financial aid form by calling the toll-free number that was mentioned earlier: (800) 4FED-AID.

To apply for other aid in addition to federal aid, you may need additional forms. High school guidance counselors can tell you more about applying for financial aid, including where to get forms you might need for state aid.

From information you report on the financial aid forms, your expected family contribution (EFC) is calculated. The EFC is the amount of money a student and his or her family is expected to contribute to the costs of attending college. Using the EFC and other information that you provide, each college to which you apply will determine your financial need. Financial need equals the cost of education minus the EFC and represents the maximum amount of need-based aid the student can receive. In addition, students can borrow money to cover the EFC.

Because financial aid determinations consider both financial need and education cost, you should not rule out a school because you think it costs too much. In fact, with financial aid it may cost no more to attend an expensive institution than a cheaper one.

How Much Need-based Financial Aid Can My Child Get?

The amount of need-based financial aid a student qualifies for depends on his or her financial need. Financial need is equal to the cost of education (estimated cost for college attendance and basic living expenses) minus the family contribution (the amount a family is expected to pay, which varies according to the family's financial resources).

Are There Other Ways To Keep The Cost Of College Down?

Serve In AmeriCorps:

AmeriCorps is a domestic Peace Corps in which thousands of young people are working in community service projects around the country in exchange for a living allowance averaging $7,500 per year, health care, child care when needed, and an education award of $4,725 per year for paying back a student loan or for financing postsecondary education. Under some circumstances a person can serve part time and receive an education award of $2,362 per year.

AmeriCorps projects serve communities throughout the country. All meet at least one of four national priorities:

1) Education.
2) Public safety.
3) Human needs.
4) The environment.

For example, AmeriCorps members teach state-of-the-art computer skills to teenagers, tutor grade-school children in basic reading, or organize innovative after-school programs in some of the education projects. AmeriCorps members in environmental projects clean up urban streams and inland waterways, monitor dangerous trends in air quality, or test-start city-wide recycling programs.

There are many different points in a person's educational career when participation in AmeriCorps is an option: right after high school, during or after college, and during or after graduate school or occupational training. AmeriCorps members are recruited locally and nationally. To find out more about AmeriCorps, call the AmeriCorps Hotline free of charge at (800) 94-ACORPS (1-800-942-2677) or TDD (800) 833-3722.

Take Advanced Placement (AP) Courses And Exams In High School:

As discussed in an earlier section, many high schools offer Advanced Placement (AP) courses and exams. AP courses are college-level courses that help students prepare for college-level work. After taking AP courses, students can take AP exams offered in the same subjects as the AP courses. If students score a grade of 3 or higher on an AP exam, they can often receive college credit. Students with high grades on AP exams in many different subjects are sometimes granted a full year of course credit at the colleges where they enroll. The receipt of course credit can result in saving in college costs. These savings can be quite large if it means that a student is able to place into a college as a second-year student; such a student might save the cost of tuition and fees for a whole year of college.

However, not all colleges and universities give college credit for a grade of 3 or higher on an AP exam. Contact your child's high school to find out if AP courses and exams are offered.

Write to the admissions office of the colleges that are of interest to your child to find out if they give credit for an AP exam grade of 3 or higher. For more information on AP courses and exams, see the address and phone number on the following page.

Participate In A Career-Focused Educational Program Such As "Tech Prep" Or "School-To-Career":

As discussed earlier, some high schools offer career-focused educational programs that provide students with a set of high school courses that are formally linked to courses offered at local community or technical colleges. These "tech-prep" or "school-to-career" programs, as they are often called, offer students the opportunity to go through a sequence of career-focused courses in high school that prepares them for an apprenticeship program or for a specialized sequence of college courses in a particular occupational field. Thus, students who master certain technical and occupational skills and knowledge in high school do not need to repeat the same courses when they enter college or an apprenticeship.

In some of these programs, students who take the special sequence of courses in high school can sometimes be awarded college credit or advanced standing in the occupational program at the college level. This can save students time and money. It also means that students can gain access to more advanced college courses much earlier in their college careers. To find out if such career-focused programs exist in your community, ask your child's guidance counselor or teacher, or staff at a local college. To learn more about career-focused programs like "tech-prep" and "school-to-career" programs, contact the organizations listed in the following section.

Enroll In A Two-Year College; Then Transfer To A Four-Year College:

Local community colleges are usually the least expensive. In addition to low tuition, they are located in the area in which the student lives, which makes it possible to save by living at home and commuting to campus.

After completing an associate's degree or certificate in a two-year college, students often can transfer to a four-year college and work toward a bachelor's degree.

If your child chooses this route, he or she needs to take courses in the two-year college that will count toward a bachelor's degree. Certain community college courses may not be transferable to a four-year institution. Community college admissions officers can explain transfer terms and opportunities.

Work Part Time:

Some students choose to work part time and attend college part time. If your child wishes to do this, he or she should make sure that work, classes, and time for studying do not conflict. Some institutions offer programs that enable students to combine work and classes. Although going to school part time is a good option for many students, it usually takes longer for part time students to earn their degrees.

Take Advantage Of Armed Forces Education Programs:

The armed forces offer educational programs during or after active duty. If your child prefers to work toward a college degree immediately after high school, attending one of the military academies or attending a civilian school and enrolling in the Reserve Officers Training Corps (ROTC) program are options. If your child wants to join the armed forces before attending college full time, he or she can attend college after military service by taking advantage of the Montgomery GI Bill or by obtaining college credit for some of the military training he or she will receive.

Military Academies:

Each branch of the military, with the exception of the Marine Corps, has its own academy — a four-year college that offers a bachelor's degree and, a commission in the military upon graduation. The military academies are highly competitive and are tuition-free to students who are admitted. The three main military academies are:

1) U.S. Military Academy, located in West Point, New York.

2) U.S. Naval Academy, located in Annapolis, Maryland.

3) U.S. Air Force Academy, located in Colorado Springs, Colorado.

Other Academies:

Two other academies operate in the same model as the military academies, with subsidized tuition in return for service. They are:

1) U.S. Coast Guard Academy, located in new London, Connecticut.

2) U.S. Merchant Marine Academy, located in Kings Point, New York.

ROTC:

In the ROTC scholarship program, the military covers most of the cost of tuition, fees, and textbooks and also provides a monthly allowance. Scholarship recipients participate in summer training while in college and fulfill a service commitment after college.

The Montgomery GI Bill:

This bill provides financial support for people who wish to pursue a college education after serving in the military.

Other Ways To Get A College Education In The Armed Forces:

Most branches of the military offer some kind of tuition assistance program that enables members to take college courses at civilian colleges during their off-duty hours while on active duty. In addition, military training while on active duty can sometimes count toward college credit. All branches of the military offer training in various technical and vocational areas, and military enrollees can obtain college credit for some of this training.

The National Guard and the Reserves offer the same kind of educational benefits as those available to people on Active Duty.

Local armed forces recruiting offices can provide detailed information about education opportunities through the military.

E) Long-Range Planning

How Do I Set Up A Long-Range Plan?

Step by step, you can help your child make informed decisions about his or her education, do well academically, learn about colleges, and find the opportunities for a college education.

Following are two checklist that are designed to help you and your child, year by year, progress toward preparing for college — both academically and financially. The first list speaks directly to your child, although he or she may need your help. The second list speaks directly to you.

College Preparation Checklist For Students

Pre-High School:

1) Take challenging classes in English, mathematics, science, history, geography, the arts, and a foreign language.

2) Develop strong study skills.

3) Start thinking about which high school classes will best prepare you for college.

4) If you have an opportunity to choose among high schools, or among different programs within one high school, investigate the options and determine which ones will help you further your academic and career interests and open doors to many future options.

5) Investigate different ways to save money — buying a U.S. Savings Bond or opening a savings account in a bank, investing in mutual funds, etc.

6) Start saving for college if you haven't already.

High School:
9th Grade

1) Taking challenging classes in English, mathematics, science, history, geography, a foreign language, government, civics, economics, and the arts.

2) Get to know your career counselor or guidance counselor, and other college resources available in your school.

3) Talk to adults in a variety of professions to determine what they like and dislike about their jobs and what kind of education is needed for each kind of job.

4) Continue to save for college.

10th Grade:

1) Take challenging classes in English, mathematics, science, history, geography, a foreign language, government, civics, economics, and the arts.

2) Talk to adults in a variety of professions to determine what they like and dislike about their jobs, and what kind of education is needed for each kind of job.

3) Become involved in school-or community-based extracurricular (before or after school) activities that interest you and/or enable you to explore career interests.

4) Meet with your career counselor or guidance counselor to discuss colleges and their requirements.

5) Take the Preliminary Scholastic Assessment Test/National Merit Scholarship Qualifying Test (PSAT/NMSQT). You must register early. If you have difficulty paying the registration fee, see your guidance counselor about getting a fee waiver.

6) Take advantage of opportunities to visit colleges and talk to students.

7) Continue to save for college.

11th Grade:

1) Take challenging classes in English, mathematics, science, history, geography, a foreign language, government, civics, economics, and the arts.

2) Meet with your career counselor or guidance counselor to discuss colleges and their requirements.

3) Continue involvement in school-or community-based extracurricular activities.

4) Decide which colleges most interest you. Write these schools to request information and an application for admission. Be sure to ask about special admissions requirements, financial aid, and deadlines.

5) Talk to college representatives at college fairs.

6) Take advantage of opportunities to visit colleges and talk to students.

7) Consider people to ask for recommendations — teachers, counselors, employers, etc.

8) Investigate the availability of financial aid from federal, state, local, and private sources. Call the student Aid Hotline at the U.S. Department of Education (1-800-4FED-AID) for a student guide to federal financial aid. Talk to your guidance counselor for more information.

9) Find out more about the domestic Peace Corps, called AmeriCorps, by calling 1-800-942-2677 or TDD 1-800833-3722.

10) Investigate the availability of scholarships provided by organizations such as corporations, labor unions, professional associations, religious organizations, credit unions.

11) If applicable, go to the library and look for directories of scholarships for women, minorities, and disabled students.

12) Register for and take the Scholastic Assessment Test (SAT 1), the ACT, SAT 2 Subject Tests, or any other exams required for admission to the colleges you might want to attend. If you have difficulty paying the registration fee, see your guidance counselor about getting a fee waiver.

13) Continue to save for college.

12th Grade:

1) Take challenging classes in English, mathematics, science, history, geography, a foreign language, government, civics, economics, the arts, and advanced technologies.

2) Meet with your counselor early in the year to discuss your plans.

3) Complete all necessary financial aid forms. Make sure that you fill out at lease one form that can be used for Federal aid.

4) Write colleges to request information and applications for admission. Be sure to ask about financial aid, admissions requirements, and deadlines.

5) If possible, visit the colleges that most interest you.

6) Register for and take the Scholastic Assessment Test (SAT 1), American College Test (ACT), SAT 2 Subject Tests, or any other exams required for admission to colleges to which you are applying. If you have difficulty paying the registration fee, see your guidance counselor about getting a fee waiver.

7) Prepare your application carefully. Follow the instructions, and PAY CLOSE ATTENTION TO DEADLINES! Be sure to ask your counselor and teachers at least two weeks before your application deadlines to submit the necessary documents to colleges (your transcript, letters of recommendation, etc.).

Financial Preparation Checklist For Parents Pre-High School:

1) Investigate different ways to save money — buying U.S. Savings Bonds or opening a savings account in a bank, etc.

2) Start saving money for your child's college education.

High School:
9th Grade:

1) Continue to save for college.

10th Grade:

1) Continue to save for college.

11th Grade:

1) Help your child investigate the availability of financial aid from federal state, local,

and private sources. Call the Student Aid Hotline at the U.S. Department of Education (1-800-4FED-AID) for a student guide to federal financial aid. Have your child talk to his or her guidance counselor for more information.

2) Help your child investigate the availability of scholarships provided by organizations such as corporations, labor unions, professional associations, religious organizations, and credit unions.

3) If applicable, go to the library with your son or daughter and look for directories on scholarships for women, minorities, and disabled students.

12th Grade

1) Make sure your child completes all necessary financial aid forms. Be sure that he or she completes at least one form that can be used for federal aid.

2) Continue to save for college.

F) Other Sources Of Information

Where Can I Get More Information On The Topics Discussed In This Book?

In this section you will find phone numbers, mailing addresses, internet addresses, and books that you can use to get more information about planning for college both financially and academically. You should be able to find most of these books and others like them at your library.

Books and Other Resources On Occupations and Careers:

1) The Occupational Outlook Handbook, 1996-97 Edition. U.S. Department of Labor, Bureau of Labor Statistics, 1996.

2) Careers for the '90s: Everything You Need To Know to find the Right Career. Research and Education Association, 1994.

3) The College Board Guide to Jobs and Career Planning, Second Edition, Joyce Slaton Mitchell. The College Board, 1994.

4) What Color is your Parachute 1996?, Richard Nelson Bolles. Ten Speed Press, 1995.

5) ACT (American College Testing) and the National Career Development Associa-

tion have developed a career exploration and guidance kit called Realizing the Dream.

Many schools around the country are using this kit to help students identify careers

of interest. Ask your child's guidance counselor if Realizing the Dream is being

used in your child's school or district. To find out more about the kit, you can call

(319) 337-1379 or write to the following address:

Heidi Hallberg
Program Coordinator
ACT
2201 North Dodge Street
P.O. Box 168
Iowa City, IA 52243-0168

Books About Choosing A College:

1) The College Guide for Parents, Third Edition, Charles Shields. The College Board, 1994.

2) Peterson's Guide to Four-Year Colleges, 1996, Twenty-Sixth Edition. Peterson's Guides, 1995.

3) Barron's Profiles of American Colleges, Twenty-First Edition. Barron's Educational Series, Inc., 1996.

4) The Multicultural Student's Guide to the Colleges, Robert Mitchell. Noonday Press, 1996.

Information About Advanced Placement (AP) Courses and Exams:

For more information, write or call:

AP Services
P.O. Box 6671
Princeton, NJ 08541-6671
Phone: (609) 771-7300 (TTY) (609) 882-4118
Fax: (609) 530-0482
E-mail: apexams@ets.org

Information About "School-to-Career" and "Tech-Prep" Programs:

For information about "School-to-Career" or "School-to-Work" programs, write

or call:

School-to-Work Opportunities information Center
400 Virginia Avenue, SW, Room 210
Washington, DC 20024
Phone: (202) 401-6222

For information about "Tech-Prep" and "2+2" programs, write or call:

National Tech Prep Network
P.O. Box 21689
Waco, TX 76702-1689
Phone: (800) 972-2766

Or:

Center for Occupational Research and Development
601 Lake Air Drive
Waco, TX 76710
Phone: (817) 772-8756

Information About Take Standardized Test:

1) The Scholastic Assessment Test (SAT 1) and the SAT 2 Subject Tests. Write or call:

   SAT Program
   P.O. Box 6200
   Princeton, NJ 08541-6200
   Phone: (609) 771-7600

2) The ACT. Write or call:

   ACT Registration
   P.O. Box 414
   Iowa City, IA 52243
   Phone: (319) 337-1270

3) The Preliminary Scholastic Assessment Test/National Merit Scholarship Qualify-

   ing Test (PSAT/NMSQT). Write or call:

   PSAT/NMSQT
   P.O. Box 6720
   Princeton, NJ 08541-6720
   Phone: (609) 771-7070

Books About Preparing for Standardized Tests:

Note: One of the best ways to prepare for standardized tests is to practice with actual tests. The first two books in the following list focus on copies of previously administered tests.

1) Real SATs. The College Board, 1995. and Official Guide to the ACT Assessment, Harcourt Brace Press, 1990.

2) Barron's How to Prepare for the ACT, Tenth Edition, George Ehrenhaft, Robert Lehrman, and Allan Mundsack. Barron's Educational Series, 1995.

3) Word Smart: Building an Educated Vocabulary, Adam Robinson. Princeton Review, 1993.

4) Preparation for the SAT, 1997 Edition, Edward Deptula (ed.). Arco Publishers, 1996.

Books About Financing Your Child's Education:

1) Paying for College: A Guide for Parents, Gerald Krefetz. The College Board, 1995.

2) College Cost and Financial Aid Handbook, 1996, Sixteenth Edition. The College Board, 1995.

3) College Scholarships & Financial Aid, Sixth Edition, John Schwartz (ed.). Arco Publishers, 1995.

Information About U.S. Savings Bonds:

Write to:

Office of Public Affairs
U.S. Savings Bonds Division
Washington, DC 20226

Information About Federal Student Financial Aid:

Request The Student Guide by writing to:

Federal Student Aid Information Center
P.O. Box 84
Washington, DC 20044

Call the Federal Student Financial Aid Information Center toll free at

1-800-4FED-AID

Books About Private Sources of Financial Aid:

1) Foundation Grants to Individuals, Ninth Edition, L. Victoria Hall (ed.). The Foundation Center, 1995.

2) The A's and B's of Academic scholarships, 1996-97, Eighteenth Edition, Deborah L. Wexler (ed.). Octameron Associates, 1995.

3) The Scholarship Book, Fifth Edition, Daniel Cassidy. Prentice Hall, Inc., 1996.

4) The Complete Grants Sourcebook for Higher Education, Third Edition, David Bauer and David Bower. Oryx Press, 1995.

Information About Educational Standards:

You can contact your child's school, the school district, or the state department of education to find out about the setting of educational standards in your community and state. The following are other sources of information:

Council of Chief State School Officers
1 Massachusetts Avenue, NW Suite 700
Washington, DC 20001-1431
Phone: (202) 408-5505

Council for Basic Education
1319 F Street NW
Washington, DC 20004
Phone: (202) 347-4171

The following associations and organizations are coordinating the development of voluntary standards:

Math:
National Council of Teachers Mathematics
1906 Association Drive
Reston, VA 22091
Phone: (800) 235-7566

Arts:
Music Educators National Conference
1806 Robert Fulton Drive
Reston, VA 22091
Phone: (800) 828-0229

Civics and Government:
Center for Civic Education
5146 Douglas Fir Road
Calabasas, CA 91302
Phone: (800) 350-4223

Foreign Language:
American Council on the Teaching of Foreign Languages
6 Executive Boulevard
Yonkers, NY 10701-6801
Phone: (914) 963-8830

Geography:
National Geographic Society
P.O. Box 1640
Washington, DC 20013-1640
Phone: (800) 368-2728

Science:
National Research Council
National Science Education Standards Project
2101 Constitution Avenue, NW
Washington, DC 20418
Phone: (202) 334-1399

Publications On Educational Standards:

1) Making Standards Matter: A Fifty-State Progress Report on Efforts to Raise Aca-

demic Standards. American Federation of Teachers, Educational Issues Department.
Washington, DC, 1995.

2)   Continuing the Commitment: Essential Components of a Successful Education Sys-
     tem. The Business Roundtable. Education Public Policy Agenda. Washington, DC,
     May 1995.

Information About AmeriCorps:

For information about AmeriCorps, call:
(800) 94-ACORPS (1-800-942-2677) or TDD (800) 833-3722

Information About Opportunities In The Armed Forces:

1)   The U.S. Army: Call (800) USA-ARMY

2)   The U.S. Air Force: Call (800) 423-USAF

3)   The U.S. Navy: Call (800) USA-NAVY

4)   The U.S. Marines: Call (800) MARINES

5)   The U.S. Coast Guard: Call (800) 424-8883

6)   The U.S. Army Reserve: Call (800) USA-ARMY

7)   The U.S. Navy Reserve: Call (800) USA-USNR

8)   The U.S. Air Force Reserve: Call (800) 257-1212

9)   The U. S. Army National Guard: Call (800) 638-7600

10) The ROTC: Call (800) USA-ROTC

Information Available Through the Internet About Planning for College:

In addition to this publication and other printed materials, a host of information
about preparing for college is available through the internet — the international network of computers that are joined by telecommunications links. People can easily share
information over the internet without having to learn computer languages. Many families have access to the internet through their schools or public libraries; some families
have a connection to the internet from a home computer.

Below you will find a short discussion of several sources of information, along
with their "addresses" on the internet. In the event that the "address" of a source changes,
you should be able to locate information about preparing for college by searching with

the use of phrases such as "college planning" or "preparing for college," or by searching

with the name of the source instead of the internet address.

Sources of Information:

1) Yahoo:

One of the large directories of information on the internet is Yahoo. Yahoo has an

information page on education and has additional pages with information about prepar-

ing for college and about paying for college.

Address: http://www.yahoo.com/Education

2) The Texas Guaranteed Student Loan Corporation (TGSLC):

The Texas Guaranteed Student Loan Corporation (TGSLC) makes a great deal of

information available to help prospective college students prepare for college. Its in-

formation includes career planning and college selection information. The name of its

internet site is Adventures in Education.

Address: http://www.tgslc.org

3) The Illinois Student Aid Commission (ISAC):

The Illinois Student Aid Commission (ISAC) also provides information over the

internet about preparing and paying for college.

Address: http://www.isac1.org

4) The Financial Aid Information Page:

The Financial Aid Information Page provides links to sources of information about

student financial aid.

Address:http://www.cs.cmu.edu/afs/cs/user/mkant/Public/FinAid/finaid. html

5) The College Board:

The College Board is a national membership association of schools and colleges

whose aim is to facilitate the student transition to higher education. Use the address

below to access information offered by the College Board.

Address: http://www.collegeboard.org

6) The Student Loan Marketing Association (Sallie Mae):

The Student Loan Marketing Association (Sallie Mae) is a provider of financial

services and operational support for higher education. Use the address below to access

information offered by Sallie Mae on planning for college.

Address: http://www.salliemae.com

7) **The U.S. Department Of Education:**

The U.S. Department of Education and its Office of Postsecondary Education have information that may be of use to you. The Student Guide is available over the internet from the Education Department. U.S. Department of Education (ED)

> Address: http://www.ed.gov

> ED's Office of Postsecondary Education
> Address: http://www.ed.gov/offices/OPE/index.html

> The Student Guide
> Address: http://www.ed.gov/prog_info/SFA/ Student Guide

Information About Opportunities In Each State:

For information about state financial aid and colleges and universities in specific states, contact the agencies listed below. They can provide you with other contacts in the State for more information.

ALABAMA
Executive Director Commission on Higher Education
100 North Union Street
Montgomery, Alabama 36104-3702
(334) 242-1998
FAX: (334) 242-0268

ALASKA
Executive Director
Alaska Commission on Post-secondary Education
3030 Vintage Boulevard
Juneau, Alaska 99801-7109
(907) 465-2962 FAX: (907) 465-5316

President
University of Alaska System
202 Butrovich Building
Fairbanks, Alaska 99775-5560
(907) 474-7311 FAX: (907) 474-7570

ARIZONA
Executive Director
Arizona Board of Regents
2020 North Central, Suite 230
Phoenix Arizona 85004
(602) 229-2500 FAX: (602) 229-2555

ARKANSAS
Director Department of Higher Education
114 East Capitol
Little Rock, Arkansas 72201
(501) 324-9300 FAX: (501) 324-9308

CALIFORNIA
Executive Director
California Postsecondary Education Commission
1303 J Street, 5th Floor
Sacramento, California 95814-2938
(916) 445-1000 FAX: (916) 327-4417
California Student Aid Commission
P.O. Box 510845
Sacramento, California 94245-0845
(916) 445-0880 FAX: (916) 327-6599

COLORADO
Executive Director
Commission on Higher Education
1300 Broadway, 2nd Floor
Denver, Colorado 80203
(303) 866-4034 FAX: (303) 860-9750

Information About Opportunities In Each State:

CONNECTICUT

Commissioner of Higher Education
Department of Higher Education
61 Woodland Street
Hartford, Connecticut 06105
(203) 566-5766 FAX: (203) 566-7865

DELAWARE

Executive Director
Delaware Higher Education
Commission
820 French Street, 4th Floor
Wilmington, Delaware 19801
(302) 577-3240 FAX: (302) 577-6765

DISTRICT OF COLUMBIA

Chief
Office of Postsecondary Education
Research and Assistance
2100 M.L. King Jr. Avenue, S.E. #401
Washington, D.C. 20020
(202) 727-3685 FAX: (202) 727-2739

FLORIDA

Executive Director
Postsecondary Education Planning
Commission
Florida Education Center
Collins Building
Tallahassee, Florida 32399-0400
(904) 488-7894 FAX: (904) 922-5388
Office of Student Financial Assistance
Room 255, Collins Building
Tallahassee, Florida 32399-0400
(904) 488-1034 FAX (904) 488-3612

GEORGIA

Chancellor
Board of Regents
University System of Georgia
244 Washington Street, S.W.
Atlanta, Georgia 30334
(404) 656-2202 FAX: (404) 657-6979

Georgia Student Finance Commission
2082 East Exchange Place
Tucker, Georgia 30084
(770) 414-3200 FAX: (770) 4143163

HAWAII

President
University of Hawaii System
2444 Dole Street
Bachman Hall, Room 202
Honolulu, Hawaii 96822
(808) 956-8207 FAX: (808) 956-5286

Hawaii State Postsecondary Education
Commission
2444 Dole Street
Bachman Hall, Room 209
Honolulu, Hawaii 96822
(808) 956-8213 FAX: (808) 956-5156

IDAHO

Executive Director for Higher
Education
State Board of Education
P.O. Box 83720
Boise, Idaho 83720-0037
(208) 334-2270 FAX: (208) 334-2632

ILLINOIS

Executive Director Board of Higher
Education
4 West Old Plaza, Room 500
Springfield, Illinois 62701
(217) 782-2551 FAX: (217) 782-8548

Illinois Student Assistance Commission
Executive Offices
500 West Monroe Street, Third Floor
Springfield Illinois 62704
(217) 782-6767 FAX: (217) 524-1858

INDIANA

Commissioner for Higher Education
Commission for Higher Education
101 West Ohio Street, Suite 550
Indianapolis, Indiana 46204-971
(317) 464-4400 FAX: (317) 464-4410

State Student Assistance Commission of
Indiana
150 West Market Street, Suite 500
Indianapolis, Indiana 46204
(317) 232-2350 FAX: (317) 232-3260

Information About Opportunities In Each State:

IOWA

Executive Director
State Board of Regents
Old Historical Building
East 12th & Grand Avenue
Des Moines, Iowa 50319
(515) 281-3934 FAX: (515) 281-6420

Iowa College Student Aid Commission
200 Tenth Street, 4th Floor
Des Moines, Iowa 50309
(515) 281- 3501 FAX: (515) 242-5996

KANSAS

Executive Director
Kansas Board of Regents
700 SW Harrison, Suite 1410
Topeka, Kansas 66603-3760
(913) 296-3421 FAX: (913) 296-0983

KENTUCKY

Executive Director
Council on Higher Education
1024 Capitol Center Drive, Suite 320
Frankfort, Kentucky 40601-8204
(502) 573-1555 FAX: (502) 573-1535

Kentucky Higher Education Assistance
Authority
1050 U.S. 127 South
Frankfort, Kentucky 40601
(502) 564-7990 FAX: (502) 564-7103

LOUISIANA

Commissioner
Board of Regents
150 Third Street, Suite 129
Baton Rouge, Louisiana 70801-1389
(504) 342-4253 FAX: (504) 342-9318

Office of Student Financial Assistance
Louisiana Student Financial Assistance
Commission
P.O. Box 91202
Baton Rouge, Louisiana 70821-9202
(504) 922-1011. FAX: (504) 922-1089

MAINE

Chancellor
University of Maine System
107 Maine Avenue
Bangor, Maine 04401-4380
(207) 973-3205 FAX: (207) 947-7556

Financial Authority of Maine
Maine Education Assistance Division
One Weston Court
State House, Station 119
Augusta, Maine 04333
(207) 287-2183 FAX: (207) 287-2233
or 628-8208

MARYLAND

Secretary of Higher Education
Maryland Higher Education
Commission
16 Francis Street
Annapolis, Maryland 21401-1781
(410) 9742971 FAX: (401) 974-3513

MASSACHUSETTS

Chancellor Higher Education
Coordinating
Council McCormark Building
1 Ashburton Place, Room 1401
Boston, Massachusetts 02108-1696
(617) 727-7785 FAX: (617) 727-6397
Massachusetts State Scholarship Office
330 Stuart Street
Boston, Massachusetts 02116
(617) 727-9420 FAX: (617) 727-0667

MICHIGAN

Michigan Higher Education
Student Loan Authority
State Department of Education
P.O. Box 30057
Lansing, Michigan 48909
(517) 373-3662 FAX: (517) 335-6699

Michigan Higher Education Assistance
Authority
P.O. Box 30462
Lansing, Michigan 48909
(517) 373-3394 FAX: (517) 335-5984

Information About Opportunities In Each State:

MINNESOTA
Executive Director Higher Education
Services Office
400 Capital Square Building
550 Cedar Street
St. Paul, Minnesota 55101
(612) 296-9665 FAX: (612) 297-8880

MISSISSIPPI
Commissioner
Board of Trustees of State Institutions
of Higher Learning
3825 Ridgewood Road
Jackson, Mississippi 39211-6453
(601) 982-6611 FAX: (601) 364-2862

MISSOURI
Commissioner of Higher Education
Coordinating Board for Higher
Education
3515 Amazonas
Jefferson City, Missouri 65109
(314) 751-2361 FAX: (314) 751-6635

MONTANA
Commissioner of Higher Education
Montana University System
2500 Broadway
Helena, Montana 59620-3101
(406) 444-6570 FAX: (406) 444-1469

NEBRASKA
Executive Director
Coordinating Commission for
Postsecondary Education
P.O. Box 95005
Lincoln, Nebraska 68509-5005
(404) 471-2847 FAX: (404) 471-2886

NEVADA
Chancellor
University of Nevada System
2601 Enterprise Road
Reno, Nevada 89512
(702) 784-1127

Nevada Department of Education
700 East 5th Street, Capitol Complex
Carson City, Nevada 89710
(702) 687-5915 FAX: (702) 687-5660

NEW HAMPSHIRE
Executive Director
New Hampshire Postsecondary
Education Commission
Two Industrial Park Drive
Concord, New Hampshire 03301-8512
(603) 271-2555 FAX: (603) 271-2696

Chancellor
University System of New Hampshire
Dunlap Center, 25 Concord Road
Durham, New Hampshire 03824-3545
(603) 868-1800 FAX: (603) 868-3021

NEW JERSEY
New Jersey Department of Higher
Education office of Student
Assistance and information Systems
4 Quakerbridge Plaza, CN 540
Trenton, New Jersey 08625
(800) 792-8670 (609) 584-9618
FAX: (609) 588-2228

NEW MEXICO
Executive Director
Commission on Higher Education
1068 Cerrillos Road
Santa Fe, New Mexico 87501-4295
(505) 827-7383 FAX: (505) 827-7392

NEW YORK
Deputy Commissioner for Higher and
Professional Education
Room 5B28 Cultural Education Center
New York State Education Department
Albany, New York 12230
(518) 474-5851 FAX: (518) 486-2175

The New York State Higher Education
Corporation
99 Washington Avenue
Albany, New York 12255
(518) 473-0431 FAX: (518) 474-2839

Information About Opportunities In Each State:

NORTH CAROLINA
Vice President for Planning
University of North Carolina
General Administration
P.O. Box 2688
Chapel Hill, North Carolina
27515-2688
(919) 962-6981 FAX: (919) 962-0488

North Carolina State Education
Assistance Authority (NCSEAA)
P.O. Box 2688
Chapel Hill, North Carolina 27515-
2688
(919) 549-8614 FAX: (919) 549-8481

College Foundation, Inc.
P.O. Box 12100
Raleigh, North Carolina 27605
(919) 821-4771 FAX: (919) 821-3139

NORTH DAKOTA
Chancellor
North Dakota University System
600 East Boulevard Avenue
Bismarck, North Dakota 58505
(701) 328-2962 FAX: (701) 328-2961

OHIO
Chancellor Ohio Board of Regents
30 East Broad Street, 36th Floor
Columbus, Ohio 43266-0417
(614) 466-0887 FAX: (614) 466-5866

OKLAHOMA
Chancellor
State Regents for Higher Education
500 Education Building
State Capitol Complex
Oklahoma City, Oklahoma 73105
(405) 524-9100 FAX: (405) 524-9230

OREGON
Chancellor
State System of Higher Education
P.O. Box 3175
Eugene, Oregon 97403-1075
(541) 346-5700 FAX: (541) 346-5764

Oregon State Scholarship Commission
1500 Valley River Drive, Suite 100
Eugene, Oregon 97401
(541) 687-7400 FAX: (541) 687-7419

PENNSYLVANIA
Commissioner for Higher Education
State Department of Education
333 Market Street
Harrisburg, Pennsylvania 17126-0333
(717) 787-5041 FAX: (717) 783-0583

Pennsylvania Higher Education
Assistance Agency
1200 North 7th Street
Harrisburg, Pennsylvania 17102
(717) 257-2850 FAX: (717) 720-3907

PUERTO RICO
Executive Director
Council on Higher Education
Box 23400, UPR Station
San Juan, Puerto Rico 00931-3400
(809) 758-3350 FAX: (809) 763-8394

RHODE ISLAND
Commissioner of Higher Education
Office of Higher Education
301 Promenade Street
Providence, Rhode Island 02908-5720
(401) 277-6560 FAX: (401) 277-6111

Rhode Island Higher Education
Assistance Authority
560 Jefferson Boulevard
Warwick, Rhode Island 02886
(401) 736-1100 FAX: (401) 732-3541

SOUTH CAROLINA
Commissioner
Commission on Higher Education
1333 Main Street, Suite 200
Columbia, South Carolina 29201
(803) 737-2260 FAX: (803) 737-2297

South Carolina Higher Education
Tuition Grants Commission
P.O. Box 12159
Columbia, South Carolina 29211
(803) 734-1200 FAX: (803) 734-1426

Information About Opportunities In Each State:

SOUTH DAKOTA

Executive Director Board of Regents
207 East Capitol Avenue
Pierre, South Dakota 57501-3159
(605) 773-3455 FAX: (605) 773-5320

Department of Education and Cultural
Affairs
Office of the Secretary
700 Governors Drive
Pierre, South Dakota 57501-2291 (605)
773- 3134 FAX: 773-6139

TENNESSEE

Executive Director
Tennessee Higher Education
Commission
Parkway Towers, Suite 1900
404 James Robertson Parkway
Nashville, Tennessee 37243-0830
(615) 741-7562 FAX: (615) 741-6230

Tennessee Student Assistance
Corporation
Parkway Towers, Suite 1950
404 James Robertson Parkway
Nashville, Tennessee 37243-0820
(615) 741-1346 FAX: (615) 741-6101

TEXAS

Commissioner
Texas Higher Education Coordinating
Board
P.O. Box 12788
Austin, Texas 78711
(512) 483-6101 FAX: (512) 483-6169

Texas Higher Education Coordinating
Board
P.O. Box 12788
Capitol Station
Austin, Texas 78711
(512) 483-6340 FAX: (512) 483-6420

UTAH

Commissioner of Higher Education
Utah System of Higher Education
3 Triad Center, Suite 550
Salt Lake City, Utah 84180-1205
(801) 321-7101 FAX: (801) 321-7199

VERMONT

Vermont Student Assistance Corporation
P.O. Box 2000
Champlain Mill
Winooski, Vermont 05404-2601

(802) 655-9602 FAX: (802) 654-3765
Chancellor
Vermont State Colleges
P.O. Box 359
Waterbury, Vermont 05676
(802) 241-2520 FAX: (802) 241-3369

President
University of Vermont
349 Waterman Building
Burlington, Vermont 05405
(802) 656-3186 FAX: (802) 656-1363

VIRGINIA

Director
State Council of Higher Education
101 North 14th Street, 9th Floor
Richmond Virginia 23219
(804) 2252600 FAX: (804) 225-2604

WASHINGTON

Executive Director
Higher Education Coordinating Board
917 Lakeridge Way
P.O. Box 43430
Olympia, Washington 98504-3430
(360) 753-7800 FAX: (360) 753-7808

WEST VIRGINIA

Chancellor
State College System of West Virginia
1018 Kanawha Boulevard
East Charleston, West Virginia 25301
(304) 558-0699 FAX: (304) 558-1011

Chancellor
University of West Virginia System
1018 Kanawha Boulevard, East, Ste. 700
Charleston, West Virginia 25301
(304) 558-2736 FAX: (304) 558-3264

Information About Opportunities In Each State:

WISCONSIN
Higher Education Aids Board
P.O. Box 7885
Madison, Wisconsin 53707
(608) 267-2206 FAX: (608) 267-2808

President
University of Wisconsin System
1700 Van Hise Hall
1220 Linden Drive
Madison, Wisconsin 53706
(608) 262-2321 FAX: (608) 262-3985

WYOMING
The Community College Commission
2020 Carey Avenue, 8th Floor
Cheyenne, WY 82002
(307) 777-7763 FAX: (307) 777-6567

President
University of Wyoming
Box 3434
Laramie, WY 82071
(307) 766-4121 FAX: (307) 766-2271

G) Important Terms

What Terms Do I Need To Understand?

Below is a glossary of some terms that you may want to remember:

A.A: This stands for an "associate of arts" degree, which can be earned at most two-year colleges.

A.A.S.: This refers to an "associate of applied science" degree, which can be earned at some two-year colleges.

ACT: This is a test published by American College Testing. It measures a student's aptitude in English, mathematics, reading, and science reasoning. Many colleges in the South and Midwest require students to take this and submit their test scores when they apply for admission. Some colleges accept this test or the SAT 1. (See below for Explanation of SAT 1.) Most students take the ACT or the SAT during their junior or senior year of high school.

B.A. or B.S.: B.A. stands for "bachelor of arts," and B.S. stands for "bachelor of science." Both degrees can be earned at four-year colleges. Some colleges only grant B.A.s and others only grant B.S.s — it depends on the kinds of courses offered at the particular college.

Default Rate: The default rate is the percentage of students who took out federal student loans to pay their expenses but did not repay them properly.

Dividends: Dividends are payments of part of a company's earnings to people who hold stock in the company.

Expected Family Contribution (EFC): An amount, determined by a formula that is specified by law, that indicates how much of a family's financial resources should be available to help pay for school. Factors such as taxable and nontaxable income, assets (such as savings and checking accounts), and benefits (for example, unemployment or Social Security) are all considered in this calculation. The EFC is used in determining eligibility for federal need-based aid.

Fees: These are charges that cover costs not associated with the student's course load, such as cost of some athletic activities, clubs, and special events.

Financial Aid: Financial aid in this book refers to money available from various sources to help students pay for college.

Financial Aid Package: The total amount of financial aid a student receives. Federal and non-federal aid such as grants, loans, or work-study are combined in a "package" to help meet the student's need. Using available resources to give each student the best possible package of aid is one of the major responsibilities of a school's financial aid administrator.

Financial Need: In the context of student financial aid, financial need is equal to the cost of education (estimated cost for college attendance and basic living expenses) minus the expected family contribution (the amount a student's family is expected to pay, which varies according to the family's financial resources).

General Educational Development (GED) Diploma: The certificate students receive if they have passed a high school equivalency test. Students who don't have a high school diploma but who have a GED will still qualify for federal student aid.

Grant: A grant is a sum of money given to a student for the purposes of paying at least part of the cost of college. A grant does not have to be repaid.

Interest: This refers to the amount that your money earns when it is kept in a savings instrument.

Investment: In this book, an investment refers to using your money to invest in something that will enable you to earn interest or dividends over time.

Liquidity: A term that refers to how quickly you can gain access to money that you invest or deposit in some kind of savings instrument.

Loan: A loan is a type of financial aid that is available to students and to the parents of students. An education loan must be repaid. In many cases, however, payments do not begin until the student finishes school.

Merit-based Financial Aid: This kind of financial aid is given to students who meet requirements not related to financial needs. Most merit-based aid is awarded on the basis of academic performance or potential and is given in the form of scholarships or grants.

Need-based Financial Aid: This kind of financial aid is given to students who are determined to be in financial need of assistance based on their income and assets and their families, income and assets, as well as some other factors.

Open Admissions: This term means that a college admits most or all students who apply to the school. At some colleges it means that anyone who has a high school diploma or a GED can enroll. At other schools it means that anyone over 18 can enroll. "Open admissions," therefore, can mean slightly different things at different schools.

Pell Grants: These are Federal need-based grants that were given to just under 4 million students for school year 1994-95. In school year 1995-96, the maximum Pell Grant was $2,340.

Perkins Loans: This is a Federal financial aid program that consists of low-interest loans for undergraduates and graduate students with exceptional financial need. Loans are awarded by the school.

PLUS Loans: These Federal loans allow parents to borrow money for their children's college education.

Postsecondary: This term means "after high school" and refers to all programs for high school graduates, including programs at two-and four-year colleges and vocational and technical schools.

Principal: This refers to the face value or the amount of money you place in a savings instrument on which interest is earned.

Proprietary: This is a term used to describe postsecondary schools that are private and are legally permitted to make a profit. Most proprietary schools offer technical and vocational courses.

PSAT/NMSQT: This stands for the Preliminary Scholastic Assessment Test/National Merit Scholarship Qualifying Test, a practice test that helps students prepare for the Scholastic Assessment Test (SAT 1). The PSAT is usually administered to tenth or eleventh grade students. Although colleges do not see a student's PSAT/NMSQT score, a student who does very well on this test and who meets many other academic performance criteria may qualify for the National Merit Scholarship Program.

Return: Return refers to the amount of money you earn through a financial investment or savings instrument. You earn money on investments and savings instruments through interest earnings or dividends.

Risk: In reference to saving money or investing money, risk refers to the danger that the money you set aside in some kind of savings plan or investment could be worth less in the future.

ROTC: This stands for Reserve Officers Training Corps program, which is a scholarship program wherein the military covers the cost of tuition, fees, and textbooks and also provides a monthly allowance. Scholarship recipients participate in summer training while in college and fulfill a service commitment after college.

SAT 1: This stands for the Scholastic Assessment Test, which is a test that measures a student's mathematical and verbal reasoning abilities. Many colleges in the East and West require students to take the SAT 1 and to submit their test scores when they apply for admission. Some colleges accept this test or the ACT. Most students take the SAT 1 or the ACT during their junior or senior year of high school.

SAT 2 Subject Test: SAT 2 Subject Tests are offered in many areas of study including English, mathematics, many sciences, history, and foreign languages. Some colleges require students to take one or more SAT 2 Tests when they apply for admission.

Savings Instrument: In this document, savings instrument refers to any kind of savings plan or mechanism you can use to save money over time. Examples of some savings instruments are savings accounts, certificates of deposit (CDs), and money market accounts.

Scholarship: A Scholarship is a sum of money given to a student for the purposes of paying at least part of the cost of college Scholarships can be awarded to students based on students' academic achievements or on many other factors.

SEOG (Supplemental Educational opportunity Grant): This is a federal award that helps undergraduates with exceptional financial need, and is awarded by the school. The SEOG does not have to be paid back.

Stafford Loans: These are student loans offered by the federal government. There are two types of Stafford Loans — one need-based and another non-need-based. Under the Stafford Loan programs, student can borrow money to attend school and the federal government will guarantee the loan in case of default. Under the Stafford Loan programs, the combined loan limits are $2,625 for the first year, $3,500 for the second year, $5,500 for the third or more years. An undergraduate cannot borrow more than a total of $23,000.

Transcript: This is a list of all the courses a student has taken with the grades that the student earned in each course. A college will often require a student to submit his or her high school transcript when the student applies for admission to the college.

Tuition: This is the amount of money that colleges charge for classroom and other instruction and use of some facilities such as libraries. Tuition can range from a few hundred dollars per year to more than $20,000. A few colleges do not charge any tuition.

William D. Ford Federal Direct Loans: Under this new program, students may obtain federal loans directly from their college or university with funds provided by the U.S. Department of Education instead of a bank or other lender.

Work-Study Programs: These programs are offered by many colleges. They allow students to work part time during the school year as part of their financial aid package. The jobs are usually on campus and the money earned is used to pay for tuition or other college charges.